Feminist Reception Studies in a Post-Audience Age

This book makes an important return to reception studies at an exciting juncture of media distribution and modes of consumption. The editors' introduction contextualizes this new work within a long history of feminist approaches to audience research, and argues that new media forms require new methods of research that remain invested in questions of gender, sexuality, and power. The contributions are rooted in the dynamics of everyday life and present innovative approaches to media and audiences. These include investigating online contexts, transnational flows of media images, and new possibilities of self-representation and distribution. Collectively, this work provides a robust theoretical and methodological framework for understanding media reception from a feminist communication and media studies perspective. The scholars included are in the vanguard of contemporary thinking about media audiences and users of technology in what some call the 'post-audience' age.

The chapters in this book were originally published as a special issue of *Feminist Media Studies*.

Andre Cavalcante is an Assistant Professor of Media Studies and Women, Gender, and Sexuality at the University of Virginia, USA. He specializes in the study of media audiences and his work focuses on LGBTQ issues and everyday life. He is the author of the forthcoming book *Struggling for Ordinary: Media and Transgender Belonging in Everyday Life*.

Andrea Press is the William R. Kenan, Jr. Professor of Sociology and Media Studies at the University of Virginia, USA, where she is the Founding Chair of the Department of Media Studies. She served as the Executive Director of the Virginia Film Festival for three years, and has published widely on feminist media audiences. She has three forthcoming books: *Media and Class: TV, Film, and Digital Culture*; *The Routledge Handbook of Contemporary Feminism*; and *Media-Ready Feminism and Everyday Sexism*.

Katherine Sender is Professor of Media and Sexuality in the Department of Communication at the University of Michigan, USA. Her book *The Makeover: Reality Television and Reflective Audiences* (2012), as well as her other books and articles, investigates feminist and queer approaches to media reception and production.

Feminist Reception Studies in a Post-Audience Age

Returning to Audiences and Everyday Life

**Edited by
Andre Cavalcante, Andrea Press and
Katherine Sender**

LONDON AND NEW YORK

First published 2018 by Routledge

2 Park Square, Milton Park, Abingdon, Oxfordshire OX14 4RN
52 Vanderbilt Avenue, New York, NY 10017

Routledge is an imprint of the Taylor & Francis Group, an informa business

First issued in paperback 2020

Copyright © 2018 Taylor & Francis

All rights reserved. No part of this book may be reprinted or reproduced or utilised in any form or by any electronic, mechanical, or other means, now known or hereafter invented, including photocopying and recording, or in any information storage or retrieval system, without permission in writing from the publishers.

Notice:
Product or corporate names may be trademarks or registered trademarks, and are used only for identification and explanation without intent to infringe.

British Library Cataloguing in Publication Data
A catalogue record for this book is available from the British Library

ISBN13: 978-1-138-57627-8 (hbk)
ISBN13: 978-0-367-59305-6 (pbk)

Typeset in MyriadPro
by diacriTech, Chennai

Publisher's Note
The publisher accepts responsibility for any inconsistencies that may have arisen during the conversion of this book from journal articles to book chapters, namely the possible inclusion of journal terminology.

Disclaimer
Every effort has been made to contact copyright holders for their permission to reprint material in this book. The publishers would be grateful to hear from any copyright holder who is not here acknowledged and will undertake to rectify any errors or omissions in future editions of this book.

Contents

Citation Information	vii
Notes on Contributors	ix

Introduction – Feminist reception studies in a post-audience age: returning to audiences and everyday life 1
Andre Cavalcante, Andrea Press and Katherine Sender

1 Lemony Liz and likable Leslie: audience understandings of feminism, comedy, and gender in women-led television comedies 14
Robyn Stacia Swink

2 *Orange Is the New Black:* the popularization of lesbian sexuality and heterosexual modes of viewing 29
Katerina Symes

3 A queerly normalized Western lesbian imaginary: online Chinese fans' gossip about the Danish fashion model Freja Beha Erichsen 42
Jing Jamie Zhao

4 Leave a comment: mommyblogs and the everyday struggle to reclaim parenthood 59
Linda Steiner and Carolyn Bronstein

5 MirrorCameraRoom: the gendered multi-(in)stabilities of the selfie 77
Katie Warfield

6 Fifty shades of consent? 93
Francesca Tripodi

Index 109

Citation Information

The chapters in this book were originally published in *Feminist Media Studies*, volume 17, issue 1 (February 2017). When citing this material, please use the original page numbering for each article, as follows:

Introduction
Feminist reception studies in a post-audience age: returning to audiences and everyday life
Andre Cavalcante, Andrea Press and Katherine Sender
Feminist Media Studies, volume 17, issue 1 (February 2017) pp. 1–13

Chapter 1
Lemony Liz and likable Leslie: audience understandings of feminism, comedy, and gender in women-led television comedies
Robyn Stacia Swink
Feminist Media Studies, volume 17, issue 1 (February 2017) pp. 14–28

Chapter 2
Orange Is the New Black: *the popularization of lesbian sexuality and heterosexual modes of viewing*
Katerina Symes
Feminist Media Studies, volume 17, issue 1 (February 2017) pp. 29–41

Chapter 3
A queerly normalized Western lesbian imaginary: online Chinese fans' gossip about the Danish fashion model Freja Beha Erichsen
Jing Jamie Zhao
Feminist Media Studies, volume 17, issue 1 (February 2017) pp. 42–58

Chapter 4
Leave a comment: mommyblogs and the everyday struggle to reclaim parenthood
Linda Steiner and Carolyn Bronstein
Feminist Media Studies, volume 17, issue 1 (February 2017) pp. 59–76

Chapter 5
MirrorCameraRoom: the gendered multi-(in)stabilities of the selfie
Katie Warfield
Feminist Media Studies, volume 17, issue 1 (February 2017) pp. 77–92

CITATION INFORMATION

Chapter 6
Fifty shades of consent?
Francesca Tripodi
Feminist Media Studies, volume 17, issue 1 (February 2017) pp. 93–107

For any permission-related enquiries please visit:
http://www.tandfonline.com/page/help/permissions

Notes on Contributors

Carolyn Bronstein is the Vincent de Paul Professor of Media Studies in the College of Communication at DePaul University, USA. She is the author of *Battling Pornography: The American Feminist Anti-Pornography Movement, 1976–1986* (2011) and co-editor of *Porno Chic and the Sex Wars: American Sexual Representation in the 1970s* (2016).

Andre Cavalcante is an Assistant Professor of Media Studies and Women, Gender, and Sexuality at the University of Virginia, USA. He specializes in the study of media audiences and his work focuses on LGBTQ issues and everyday life. He is the author of the forthcoming book *Struggling for Ordinary: Media and Transgender Belonging in Everyday Life*.

Andrea Press is the William R. Kenan, Jr. Professor of Sociology and Media Studies at the University of Virginia, USA, where she is the Founding Chair of the Department of Media Studies. She served as the Executive Director of the Virginia Film Festival for three years, and has published widely on feminist media audiences. She has three forthcoming books: *Media and Class: TV, Film, and Digital Culture*; *The Routledge Handbook of Contemporary Feminism*; and *Media-Ready Feminism and Everyday Sexism*.

Katherine Sender is Professor of Media and Sexuality in the Department of Communication at the University of Michigan, USA. Her book *The Makeover: Reality Television and Reflective Audiences* (2012), as well as her other books and articles, investigates feminist and queer approaches to media reception and production.

Linda Steiner is a Professor in the Philip Merrill College of Journalism at the University of Maryland, USA. The editor of *Journalism & Communication Monographs*, she is the author of a hundred journal articles and book chapters. Her co-authored or co-edited books include *Women and Journalism* (2004), *Key Concepts in Critical Cultural Studies* (2010), *Routledge Companion to Media and Gender* (2013), and the *Handbook on Gender and War* (2016).

Robyn Stacia Swink is a doctoral candidate in the Sociology Department at the University of Missouri, USA. Her areas of interest include feminist theory, cultural studies, the sociology of humour, and media studies. Her current research explores the relationships among gender, media representations, humour, and inequality with an added emphasis on audience reception of popular texts.

NOTES ON CONTRIBUTORS

Katerina Symes is a PhD candidate in the Department of Communication Studies, Concordia University, Canada. She is co-author (along with Krista Geneviève Lynes) of the entry entitled "Cyborgs and Virtual Bodies" in the *Oxford Handbook of Feminist Theory*. Her research is supported by the Social Sciences and Humanities Council of Canada.

Francesca Tripodi is a postdoctoral scholar at the Data and Society Research Institute, USA. She completed her PhD in Sociology at the University of Virginia, USA. Her research focuses on media inequality and processes of gender, race, and sexual discrimination in participatory media environments.

Katie Warfield is faculty in the Department of Journalism and Communication at Kwantlen Polytechnic University, Canada. She is director of the Visual Media Workshop, a centre for education and research into visual culture via social media. She teaches classes in communication theory, popular culture, media and diversity, and social media, and is interested in post-humanism, phenomenology, new materialism, and gender theory.

Jing Jamie Zhao is a PhD student in Film and TV Studies at the University of Warwick, UK. She has received a PhD in Gender Studies at the Chinese University of Hong Kong. Her research spans a series of topics on Chinese-speaking queer media and cyber fan cultures.

Feminist reception studies in a post-audience age: returning to audiences and everyday life

Andre Cavalcante, Andrea Press and Katherine Sender

Introduction

Joke O. K. E. Hermes recently wrote that "Qualitative audience studies have arguably been the best possible expression of feminist engagement in media studies" (2014, 61). It was the recognition that feminist audience research has been constitutive of feminist media studies that led us to edit this special issue, which re-assesses the role of feminist audience study in contemporary media research. Each of us is acutely aware of the strength of the feminist audience tradition, which has been an important influence on the research each of us has produced. Yet in our view the new media environment differs in profound ways from the media environment that gave rise to what has become known as "feminist audience study." The relationship between media and time, and the collapse of what scholars labeled the "separate spheres" between the genders, has shifted so radically that we can no longer think neatly about "women's" daytime media, or Tania Modleski's seminal notion of "women's time" (1982), both of which gave impetus to the paradigmatic early studies of soap operas and women's reception of them.

Concomitantly, we noticed that audience studies had become increasingly less visible in the pages of *Feminist Media Studies,* a paucity that represents the field of feminist media studies more generally. Carolyn M. Byerly (2016), for example, found that at a large, international gender and media studies conference in 2014, only 8 percent of presentations were based on audience research. In this special issue, we set out to prioritize feminist media audience research in the context of rapidly transforming media environments, to investigate novel methods to approach new media engagements, and to reflect on how the tradition continues to be distinctive and important in the burgeoning field of feminist media study.

Feminist audience studies' interrogation of everyday life

In 1941, Herta Herzog published what is often thought of as the first feminist audience study, the classic study of female listeners of daytime radio soap operas published as "On Borrowed Experience: An Analysis of Listening to Daytime Sketches." The first of its kind, the study centered on the role media plays in the everyday lives of ordinary women. From the one hundred interviews she conducted with women from New York, predominantly housewives, Herzog unveiled how listening to soap operas, or what her participants called "the stories," served diverse functions and offered various gratifications or pleasures, depending upon the model of reception one uses. As the title of her study suggests, Herzog maintained that listeners *borrow* the extraordinary experiences of characters on soap operas in order to, for example, feel something typically absent in their lives such as excitement or desire. Soap operas afforded listeners simple pleasures, "an element of adventure in their daily drudgery" (Herta Herzog 2004, 149). Although Herzog's analysis was steeped in psychoanalytic assumptions, trivialized the soap opera genre, and perceived its female listeners as naïve, it was nevertheless pioneering. It opened a window onto a domain overlooked by academics of the time, mainly the housewife's daily round, replete with its patterns (the routine of housework), pleasures (stolen moments to enjoy a cigarette and the radio), and frustrations (boredom and monotony). This was the study's hidden script, for it was as much about listening to the radio as it was about women's daytime everyday life. In fact, the study reveals that the two are essentially intertwined, for it was through the women's narration of their experiences with media that the texture of everyday life became intelligible.

In Herzog's time, everyday life was often profoundly gendered. For decades, feminist theorists have discussed the division of life into the "public" and the "private," ascribing the domain of the masculine to the former, and the feminine to the latter (Nancy Fraser 1985, 1990; Linda J. Nicholson 1983, 2013; Iris Marion Young 1985). Feminist media studies began during the theorization of this divide between public and private. Given the nature of radio in her time, Herzog's radio soap operas were listened to exclusively at home, in private, during the daytime. This was the domestic, private space within which, it was thought, many women of the time lived their lives—though we now know that this is a class- and race-specific assumption. Nevertheless, for early feminist media scholars, women's everyday life was visualized as taking place in a profoundly different space than that of men, who more often lived their daily lives within the public space of paid labor. Though women labored, of course, even those in the paid labor force worked an unpaid "second shift" of housework and childcare which took place within the private space of the home (and many still do, according to the research; cf. Arlie Hochschild and Anne Machung [2012] and Jerry A. Jacobs and Kathleen Gerson [2004]).

Since Herzog's study, everyday life has continued to be fertile ground for feminist and audience research and theory (Ien Ang 1985; Jacqueline Bobo 1995; Julie D'acci 1994; Dorothy Hobson 1982; Andrea L. Press 1991; Janice Radway 1984). One of the seminal texts of early feminist media audience studies built similarly on this assumption of the separate spheres. Like Herzog, Radway's (1984) ethnographic study of female romance readers found that women used their consumption of the romance novel—a profoundly gendered media product, said to appeal primarily to women—to both claim their own private leisure time within a private sphere that represented enormous labor for housewives and mothers, and to concretize their admiration for the strong female heroines who predominated in their favorite books. Romances, previously denigrated as the trash brainless housewives consumed in reflection of their lack of critical thought, were thus re-appropriated by feminist theorists as tools of escape from this drudgery.

The success of Radway's work precipitated an abundance of similarly inspired studies which collectively became known as the tradition of "feminist audience studies." Radway's publication in 1984 coincided with the rise of feminist research in the social sciences and the humanities. Often this meant simply including women as research subjects, since they had rarely been included before. Sometimes it meant employing more interpretive as opposed to more objective methods, on the theory that "difference" needed interpretation to be understood. Some even went so far as to write about "feminist methodology" as a more sensitive employing of a variety of interpretive methods to study personal issues thought particular to women and other minorities (Shulamit Reinharz and Lynn Davidman 1992).

In this new tradition of feminist audience studies, genres thought to be preferred by women were newly studied. Television soap operas, for example, were widely studied. And the division of television studies into daytime soaps (Mary Ellen Brown 1994) and prime-time soap opera programming (Hobson 1982; Sonia Livingstone Livingstone 2013; Andrea L. Press 1990) reveals a continuing tension in the feminist audience literature between those who think of everyday life in terms of feminist theory's division between the public and private spheres, and those who recognize that these spheres are and have always been porous, with both men and women weaving in and out of each realm. Some feminist audience research investigated television through this lens (David Morley 1986; Press 1991), using the methods pioneered by Hobson and Radway, but complicating the division between male and female media spheres. Andrea L. Press and Elizabeth R. Cole (1999) built upon earlier feminist media work (Fraser 1985; Angela McRobbie 1978) to investigate a gendered "semi-public" sphere for women, within which they debated political and moral issues such as abortion with friends, family, and others, but often within what were considered private spaces.

As the discipline evolved, feminist audience research also began to place the experience of lesbian, gay, bisexual, transgender, and queer communities under its purview, leading the way for the practice of queer audience research. In the 1990s, the surge of a radical queer politics motivated by the AIDS epidemic and systemic homophobia and the development of queer theory energized media scholars' interest in the work of queer audiences. Queer audience research shared feminists' interests in relations of social power, the politics of sex and gender, and the theorization of public and private spheres, but more fervently foregrounded the question of sexuality, waged a more muscular critique against structures of heteronormativity and the gender binary, and underscored the prevalence of and necessity for ideological resistance. Scholars noted that while throughout media history queer audiences had engaged with texts in complicated and creative ways, mobilizing a queer way of looking or a "queer gaze," queer theory offered a set of theoretical and discursive tools to talk about this activity. Alexander Doty (1993) argued that queer audiences had always performed queer readings of texts, reading "against the grain" and generating transgressive interpretations of media not produced with them in mind (also see Larry Gross 2001). He also argued that queer sensibility was not peripheral to media culture, but rather existed at its heart. One did not have to gaze too deeply to find queerness in popular culture.

Perhaps most evidently, queer audience research highlighted, even celebrated, the role of resistant readings. A central tenet of queer theory, the notion of resistance became a primary lens through which to examine queer spectatorship. Looking at queer slash fiction, Frederik Dhaenens, Sofie Van Bauwel, and Daniel Bitereyst (2008) argued the practice of queer audience resistance is a "politics of transgression," one that generates pleasure and hinges on "subversive or nonhegemonic articulation" (2008, 344). However, some scholars suggested that outright opposition is not always tenable or desirable. Looking at the work of queer audiences of color to uncover how they survived in a media environment organized not only around heterosexuality but also whiteness, José Esteban Muñoz (1999) advanced the idea of "disidentification." As a complicated reception practice employed by queer audiences of color, disidentification "neither opts to assimilate within a structure nor strictly opposes it; rather, [it] is a strategy that works on and against dominant ideology" (2008, 11). It is to desire and enjoy dominant media culture, but to do so tactically and "with a difference" (2008, 15). Disidentification offered a "third way" of discerning queer audience engagement within the context of an everyday life fully organized around media and communications technologies where flat out resistance is not always feasible. More recently, scholars such as Andre Cavalcante (2016) have begun to examine the phenomenology of queer audience engagement, looking to develop "a theoretical framework for thinking through quieter, less heroic, and less politically charged forms of media use, those that often go overlooked by researchers" (2016, 111).

The challenge of the contemporary media environment

In the current media moment, researchers are returning to the meanings of media and "everyday life" that were so important in early feminist audience study. To speak about everyday life is to engage with a complex knot of meanings and definitions. The term was initially denaturalized by Henri Lefebvre (1991) who saw our taken-for-granted routines as offering comfort and predictability within the industrial rhythms of the modern world. Feminist scholars recognized the gendered potential of this for understanding media reception. Everyday life is that inevitable space from which social, cultural, and political activity begins, "the unavoidable basis for all other forms of human endeavor" (Rita Felski 1999). Defined by the dynamics of repetition and familiarity, it is a routine sequence of taken-for-granted experiences. In fact, in order for everyday life to be livable, it cannot require constant and arduous thought and reflexivity, and must, at least on some level, be felt as automatic and granted. However, this unconscious, routinized nature of everyday life is both accommodating and problematic. For example, the classic feminist critique—energized by Simone de Beauvoir's (1952) "second sex," Betty Friedan's (1963) "problem that has no name," Audre Lorde's (1984) "sister outsider," and Dorothy Smith's (1987) "everyday world as problematic"—emerged directly from women's and men's conflicting experiences in everyday life. It is from within this rich earth of everyday experience—a contradictory assemblage of structure/agency, pleasure/pain, routine/rupture, and the ordinary/extraordinary—that audiences engage with media and communications technologies.

Early feminist scholarship moved from Hobson's focus on radio to a preoccupation and interest in the medium of television, which feminists placed at the center of everyday experience. Television scholar Roger Silverstone (1994) notes that television became a central feature of our daily experience in the late twentieth century because it fit so well into the temporal and spatial rhythms of everyday life. Modleski (1982) links daytime viewing, particularly of television soap operas, to the fragmented rhythm of housework. For Paddy Scannell (1996), television and radio were constitutive of everyday life because they structured our daily concerns and organized our shared world. As "world disclosing" (Scannell 1996, 161), broadcasting brought the public world into our private living rooms. Lynn Spigel's groundbreaking (1992) work noted the inherently gendered way television was defined and introduced into the American daily round. She argued that television, as *the* defining symbol of post-war domestic life, undermined paternal authority, both challenged and reinscribed conventional roles for women, and generated consumer fantasies along gendered lines. Television became central to media scholars' thinking because it offered audiences ontological security (a feeling of comfort and safety in our own skin and in the world as it is); acted as a transitional object (something that supported us through our various stages of life); and could be seamlessly integrated into our cultural myths and social rituals (Silverstone 1994).

However, the post-war era, defined as it was by television and radio, has given way to a new media environment, one where the everyday world is now fully mediatized (Stig Hjarvard 2013). Earlier feminist scholarship understood the consumption of television and radio to occur primarily in specifically gendered spaces, an assumption now open to question. Contemporary audience scholars must be prepared for a new media environment in which our earlier equation of specific media with particular "spheres" of life such as the public and private no longer makes sense. As we seamlessly and habitually migrate across media platforms, we increasingly live a "media life" where "we do not live *with*, but *in*, media" (Mark Deuze 2012, xiii). The technological character of our media life is defined by portability, interactivity, and ubiquity, along with convergence, embeddedness, and "taken-for-grant-edness" (Richard Ling 2012). Though media consumption is still gendered, we no longer employ the easy spatial equation of public/private, male/female that characterized earlier work. In fact, even the public sphere has been profoundly altered by new media, which introduced a "flow" of private and public concerns into the media experience of most users of any gender.

In this environment it is fitting that scholarship would turn toward everyday life as a privileged site of audience research and discern the role media plays in how we act out our everyday lives and subjectivities. As central components to work, leisure, and domestic life, the products of the new media ecosystem further demand and multiply our performance of self through voice, text, and image. We create an army of second selves in the digital world, distribute them across space and time, and watch others do the same. In this way, we are more fully and frequently engaged in the social processes of performing and audiencing, of self-presentation and spectatorship in everyday life (Brian Longhurst 2007). Media production is no longer the domain of the media industries proper, and media reception is no longer confined to a specific place and time. Rather, performing and audiencing happen constantly. We take selfies on the subway, and consume streaming video standing in line at the coffee shop. Gender is no longer a determinant of this behavior, although gendered differences are still observable and important.

The stuff of our everyday lives is increasingly becoming the content of our media. As more of us enter into "media life," Graeme Turner (2010) argues we have reached a "demotic turn," where the participation of ordinary people in media culture is historically unprecedented and where audience behavior is inherently interactive. Turner is careful to qualify that the demotic turn in the media industries and in our everyday lives is not necessarily or inherently "democratic." Its myriad consequences are complicated and contingent, and fail to disclose any politically progressive or coherent pattern.

This special issue directs a critical lens toward these evolving trends in media and everyday life and questions their feminist and queer implications. For example, it examines the ways the film *Fifty Shades of Grey* failed to realize the new media's potential to integrate the everyday audiences they represent into texts. It shines a light on the ways blogs, as everyday resources, help parents discursively negotiate the pressures and politics of raising children, adding to the previously highly gendered private realm of mothering a public dimension. It uncovers how online gossip, as a form of everyday talk, is deployed to both queer and further cement hetero-patriarchal norms in Chinese society. Altogether, this issue investigates the extent to which emergent media forms amplify our gendered and sexual relations in everyday life, challenge them, and introduce new ones.

The research we present here shows that, however highly interrogated a subject, gender remains relevant and important in media audience study, which continues to draw from the distinguished tradition of qualitative feminist audience research to shed light on consumption and interpretation of media in a new era. The same environment that has demanded a reconsideration of media use in everyday life also invites us to review the methods we employ to study this. How have contemporary approaches to reception built upon feminist foundations in audience research, adapted and applied to new media environments? What opportunities and challenges do these new media offer to feminist scholars researching contemporary audience formations and practices? Drawing on evolving contributions from feminism, queer theory, and critical race theory, new media practices demand innovative and ethical approaches to audience research. This volume showcases some highly original methods that address reception in increasingly complex media environments.

Revisiting qualitative methods in feminist audience research

Qualitative research methods have been seen to be both particularly illuminating for and ethically sympathetic with feminist media concerns. These methods have traditionally included fan letters (see, for example, Ang 1985), in-depth interviews (e.g., Radway 1984), telephone interviews (S. Elizabeth Bird 1992), ethnography (McRobbie 1978), and focus groups (Sut Jhally and Justin Lewis 1992; Press and Cole 1999; Radway 1984). Researchers paid attention to both text and context—using ethnographic methods to explore how people make media content meaningful to them both as content and in their domestic, familial, and other social relationships (Ann Gray 1992; Morley 1986). Methodological concerns reflected broader debates in the field, such as: How can we creatively investigate the relationships among textual determination, polysemy, and resistive readings? How can we discover how audiences make texts meaningful? How can we minimize the researcher effects inherent in participatory methods? Additionally, what constituted "feminist" methods was by no means taken for granted: What does it mean to bring a feminist politics to audiences' media reception? Are there particular ethical dilemmas that feminist commitments pose? (see, for example, Reinharz and Davidman 1992; Judith Stacey 1988).

New media do not dispense with these early questions, but frame them within the specific conditions of our contemporary media landscape. The growing complexities of convergence culture (Henry Jenkins 2006) require new ways of thinking about audiences and innovative approaches to conducting research. Our media landscape introduces amazing riches for audience researchers, but with these riches come challenges and responsibilities. The major methodological opportunities and dilemmas for audience researchers include new media's ubiquity, its multi-sited distribution, and its global spread; intersectional, reflexive, and interactive audiences; and questions of privacy and informed consent in online settings. Below we consider feminist approaches to these novel conditions and introduce some creative methodological responses to them, including those in the works presented in this special issue.

John Ellis's (2000) observation that we have experienced a radical transformation in television availability in the West from scarcity before the 1980s to abundance since the 2000s can be extended to media more generally. This is a boon but also a challenge for audience researchers; never has there been so much content, both in terms of "texts" and in terms of freely available audience-generated data about their media interactions. This massive availability brings with it primary questions about the "field" in field studies, in both spatial and temporal aspects. Where is the field? When and where do we study people's engagement with media? This abundance requires judicious delimitation through careful sampling methods that both capture the range of texts and contexts necessary to address research questions, without submitting to the temptation of "mass archiving" (Annette N. Markham 2013). Sheer volumes of materials do not guarantee diversity within them, and feminist scholars continue to pay attention to selection and focus in order to access gendered dimensions of power and experience. For example, Annemarie Navar-Gill (forthcoming) adopted a mixed-method strategy in her study of women-focused shows' writers' room twitter activity during one month in 2015. She used an automated coding process to identify major themes among sixteen thousand tweets and then focused on these themes in her fine-grained qualitative analysis.

Connected to the abundance and ubiquity of contemporary media is its multi-sitedness: audiences connect with transmedia content across a range of platforms. What are the boundaries of the field? The movements of itinerant audiences across an increasingly complex and seemingly infinite network of new media sites challenge us to consider how we trace these mobilities in rich and nuanced ways. As Andrea Press and Sonia Livingstone (2006) write, "filling in a survey to record an evening's viewing is tricky, but by no means as tricky as recording and interpreting an evening's surfing or chat" (186). Markham (2013) advocates "a more flexible notion of the field is one that allows us to stop thinking about it as an object, place, or whole—and start thinking more about movement, flow, and process" (2013, 438). How gendered audiences are mobile across different media platforms, particularly those of social media, is a fruitful approach to the multi-sitedness of our contemporary media scene (see, for example, Shayla Thiel-Stern 2013).

Multi-sited media environments are no longer contained by national boundaries, demanding that we consider how to approach the global spread of media content. Radhika Parameswaran (2013) argues that audience research should be part of broader intra- and interdisciplinary investigations of the impact of globalizing media systems, including debates about "cultural imperialism, consumerism, neoliberalism, hybridity, postcolonial class formations, gender and nationalism, emerging markets, anti-globalization movements, and multiculturalism" (2013, 10) Yet Sonia Livingstone (2003) argues that studying across cultures is hard to do well, not least because of cultural sensitivities and unequal power relationships among researchers and participants and/or collaborating researchers in different places. For example, Bryan C. Taylor and Thomas R. Lindlof (2016) discuss Aziz Douai's study of Moroccan news media audiences and his struggle to recruit women participants. Douai reflects that Moroccan women were reluctant to meet him in the café he used for interviews because to do so would be socially stigmatizing. Transnational audience research can illuminate the gendered dimensions of globalizing media networks at the same time as posing methodological challenges that illuminate structures of power that underpin local customs.

The growing complexities with which media use and everyday routines are becoming integrated demand that audience researchers reconsider the ethical challenges posed by increasingly slippery public/private spheres online. In some senses, the lower barriers to privacy and media users' familiarity with circulating relatively intimate materials in public settings is a boon for researchers (Thiel-Stern 2013). Yet the shift from the living room to more private spaces of media engagement make contextual field methods, "hanging out," more awkward (Fabienne Darling-Wolf 2013). Online spaces offer new ways to observe social interactions in and with media, for example lurking (Markham 2013). But the boundaries can be very unclear between what is considered private and public online, not only legally but among the members of a particular site, raising issues of consent, anonymity, and personal and social consequences. Parameswaran outlines

> the ethical considerations that must guide the research process, beginning with entering and monitoring chat groups and forums, procuring informed consent, ensuring a fair and dialogic exchange with the respondents, willingness to change research designs, accepting withdrawals and refusals from participants at any stage, and maintaining vigilance to protect subjects' anonymity. (2013, 9)

The power-inflected dimensions of these considerations gain additional weight for researchers committed to a feminist ethics in research.

Communication scholars have also considered methodological approaches to explore intersectionality (Kimberlé Crenshaw 1991) by investigating the complex interactions among identity categories, media reception, and power. Some early audience researchers investigated dynamics among gender and race (for example, Bobo 1995), gender, class, and age (Press 1991), and race and class (Jhally and Lewis 1992). The plethora of data available for multiply-situated audiences offer new opportunities to audience researchers to methodologically address audiences' intersectional identifications in their textual interactions. Olena Hankivsky and Daniel Grace (2015), for example,

> conceptualize ... a flexible, adaptable, and critical research strategy for moving beyond single or typically favored categories of analysis (e.g., sex, gender, race, and class) to consider simultaneous interactions between different aspects of social identity (e.g., race/ethnicity, Indigeneity, gender, class, sexuality, geography, age, ability, immigration status, and religion) and systems and processes of oppression and domination (e.g., racism, classism, sexism, ableism, and heterosexism). (2)

They suggest various methodological approaches that look at the dynamic interactions among systems of power, including institutional, group, and interpersonal contexts. Even with this welcome focus on increasingly nuanced approaches to audiences and identity position, it is notable that there is still very little research that addresses men, particularly white, privileged men, as audiences. Parameswaran (2013) notes a couple of rare exceptions, and includes a couple more in her audience studies volume, but intersectionality most often is used to describe multiply marginalized positions, leaving privilege unmarked.

New media contexts thus offer both opportunities and challenges for feminist research through changing contours of "the field," more interactive, nuanced, and reflexive ideas of "the audience," and more complex relations between these and with our own subject-positions as researchers. To what extent can traditional qualitative approaches to studying reception be repurposed in new media contexts?

Familiar methods, such as immersive fieldwork and focus group interviews have proven productive especially when considering the everyday contexts for media use. Mary L. Gray

FEMINIST RECEPTION STUDIES IN A POST-AUDIENCE AGE

(2009) undertook a deep participant observation study to investigate how rural queer youth mobilized media in conjunction with other local resources to fashion a community, however fragile, in which members could find solidarity and support. Cavalcante (2016) conducted in-depth interviews and engaged in participant observation of discussion and support groups to examine the role of media and communications technologies in the everyday lives of transgender people. In this special issue, Robyn Swink uses focus group research to address how participants wrestled with the tensions between feminism and humor in contemporary women-led comedy shows. Katarina Symes re-examines the male gaze in her textual analysis of *Orange is the New Black*. She reconsiders spectator theory to argue that the show's main protagonist, Piper Chapman, offers a "heterosexual proxy" for straight women audiences to explore same-sex desire.

Some researchers have considered the uses of conventional ethnographic methods in the context of new media environments. Radhike Gajjala, for example, asks, "Can we transpose concerns that arise out of real-life (RL) anthropology or face-to-face ethnography onto the study of virtual communities without considering seriously the very important differences in the nature of face-to-face interaction and virtual interaction?" (2004, 8). Audience scholars have devised novel ways of adapting field methods to new media environments. Adrienne Shaw (2015) spent time watching her participants play single-player video games, sometimes playing with or alongside them as they chatted, in order to understand their identifications—or not—with video game avatars. In audience research focusing on online communities—message boards, for example—Press and Livingstone (2006) note that although these come with the disadvantage of having very little contextual information in which to place participants, "the advantage is that online ethnographies are based on texts which are already written, as opposed to interview transcripts or participant observation field notes generated by the research process" (2006, 188). In this special issue, Jing Jamie Zhao creatively utilizes online gossip to investigate Chinese women's attraction to Danish model Freja Beha Erichsen in the context of Chinese values of femininity, fidelity, and family. Linda Steiner and Carolyn Bronstein analyze comments posted to controversial parenting online articles that struggled with risk, choice, and safety within the context of neoliberal parenting. Rather than treating the blogs and comments according to norms for textual analysis, on one hand, or interviews, on the other, both articles explore online content as specific cultural forms—for example, a moderated discussion not natural conversation.

Media scholars also consider novel affordances for data gathering that new media offer. Markham (2013), for example, asks, "Photography and sketching are traditional methods, but how can we reimagine these activities in social media contexts? How might we combine webcams, video recordings, screengrabs, or video screencaptures with written notes to build visually rich renderings of what is happening?" (2013, 441). In her study of the production and posting of selfies included in this special issue, Katie Warfield presents an innovative use of technologies to transform photo-elicitation in the service of self-reflexivity. Not only does she ask participants to take a series of selfies, she was interested in how participants understood the moment of image-production. In order to lessen the impact of her presence she set up a Google chat conversation while she sat and watched in another location. Warfield thus adapted conventional methods of photo-elicitation to explore the performance of selfhood in the context of what Gillian Rose calls "the hypervisuality of much contemporary everyday life" (2014, 26).

Some scholars have argued that the interactive, multi-sited nature of contemporary media engagements call for multiple and mixed methods to triangulate these increasingly complex media landscapes. Investigating gender and sexual policing on the popular website, the Anonymous Confession Board (ACB), Andrea L. Press and Francesca Tripodi (2014) found that participants were unwilling to discuss in interviews their activities there. The researchers turned to an online anonymous survey to access participants' feminist responses to posts, and followed up with a focus group to further deepen their understandings of posters' motivations and reservations regarding ACB. Katherine Sender (2012) triangulated among reality television series, online message board posts, online surveys, and telephone interviews with fans to understand the various kinds of reflexivity that audiences brought to their understanding of the makeover show genre. Others have advocated mixed methods to address the multilayered experiences of intersectionality. Hankivsky and Grace (2015), for example, recommend combining quantitative approaches that can accommodate large and heterogeneous samples with more nuanced qualitative methods that, together, can understand the multiplicative impacts of various axes of marginalization. To investigate the complex intersections of race, class, and religion among women viewers of lifestyle television, Beverley Skeggs and Helen Wood (2012) designed a multi-staged project that included micro-analysis of verbal and physical responses to watching shows (text-in-action), individual interviews, and focus group sessions. Through this multi-method approach, Skeggs and Wood found subtle differences in the articulation of "value" among the participants that reflected their intersectional experiences. In this special issue, Francesca Tripodi investigated BDSM (bondage, dominance, discipline, submission, sadism, and masochism) practitioners' critical responses to the representation of dominance, submission, and consent in the wildly popular *50 Shades of Grey* (E. L. James 2012) series. She accessed the group's ambivalent reception of the novel and new-comers' interests in BDSM by combining participant observation with a local BDSM social group, interviews with its members (some via Skype), and an analysis of discussions on online forums.

Just as the media we investigate aren't wholly new, nor are the structures in which these are produced (economic, industrial, technological, and so on); indeed, Jenkins (2006) notes that as media have become more interactive and perhaps democratic for audiences, media industry consolidation has also intensified. Similarly, the methods we apply to the phenomenon of audiences aren't wholly new, nor are the ethical considerations we need to keep in mind in our design and follow-through of research. The ubiquity, multi-sitedness, and porousness of what we can consider media "fields," along with new forms of audience activity and reflexivity offer feminist researchers new ways to investigate the gendered dimensions of media use. As with "old" media, we need in new media environments to employ feminist approaches at each stage of research: topic, context, design, recruitment, method, analysis, and distribution. Yet digital media landscapes demand that we review the ethical dimensions of feminist audience studies, including the nature of our involvement with participants, the desirability and possibility of collaboration, whose voice we hear and who has the last word, and how to protect vulnerable participants. By doing so we can reaffirm our methodological commitment to examining at all stages of research the gendered and intersectional structures of power and privilege that shape the contexts we investigate, our interactions with participants, and our writing and distribution of research. This special issue presents some of the most innovative work in audience research that centers gender and feminism to understand the changing dynamics of reception in our new media landscape.

Disclosure statement

No potential conflict of interest was reported by the authors.

References

Ang, Ien. 1985. *Watching Dallas: Soap Opera and the Melodramatic Imagination*. Translated by Della Couling. New York, NY: Methuen.

de Beauvoir, Simone. 1952. *The Second Sex*. New York: Knopf.

Bird, S. Elizabeth. 1992. *For Enquiring Minds: A Cultural Study of Supermarket Tabloids*. Memphis, TN: Univ. Of Tennessee Press.

Bobo, Jacqueline. 1995. *Black Women as Cultural Readers*. New York: Columbia University Press.

Brown, Mary Ellen. 1994. *Soap Opera and Women's Talk: The Pleasure of Resistance*. Newbury Park, CA: SAGE.

Byerly, Carolyn M. 2016. "Stasis and Shifts in Feminist Media Scholarship." In *Gender in Focus: (New) Trends in Media*, edited by C. Cerqueira, R. Cabecinhas and S. I. Magalhães, 15–27. Braga: CECS.

Cavalcante, Andre. 2016. "I Did It All Online:" "Transgender Identity and the Management of Everyday Life." *Critical Studies in Media Communication* 33 (1): 109–122. doi:10.1080/15295036.2015.1129065.

Crenshaw, Kimberlé. 1991. "Mapping the Margins: Intersectionality, Identity Politics, and Violence against Women of Color." *Stanford Law Review* 43: 1241–1299.

D'acci, Julie. 1994. *Defining Women: Television and the Case of Cagney & Lacey*. Chapel Hill: University of North Carolina Press.

Darling-Wolf, Fabienne. 2013. "Nomadic Scholarship." In *The International Encyclopedia of Media Studies*, edited by Angharad N. Valdivia, 212–231. Malden, MA: Wiley-Blackwell.

Deuze, Mark. 2012. *Media Life*. Cambridge, UK: Polity Press.

Dhaenens, Frederik, Sofie Van Bauwel, and Daniel Biltereyst. 2008. "Slashing the Fiction of Queer Theory: Slash Fiction, Queer Reading, and Transgressing the Boundaries of Screen Studies, Representations, and Audiences." *Journal of Communication Inquiry* 32 (4): 335–347. doi:10.1177/0196859908321508.

Doty, Alexander. 1993. *Making Things Perfectly Queer: Interpreting Mass Culture*. Minneapolis, MN: University of Minnesota Press.

Ellis, John. 2000. *Seeing Things: Television in the Age of Uncertainty*. New York: IB Tauris.

Felski, Rita. 1999. "The Invention of Everyday Life." *New Formations: A Journal of Culture/Theory/Politics* 39: 15–31.

Fraser, Nancy. 1985. "What's Critical about Critical Theory? The Case of Habermas and Gender." *NewGerman Critique* 35: 97–131.

Fraser, Nancy. 1990. "Rethinking the Public Sphere: A Contribution to the Critique Ofactually Existing Democracy." *Social Text* 25 (25/26): 56–80.

Friedan, Betty. 1963. *The Feminine Mystique*. New York: W.W. Norton.

Gajjala, Radhike. 2004. *Cyber Selves: Feminist Ethnographies of South Asian Women*. Walnut Creek, CA: AltaMira Press.

Gray, Ann. 1992. *Video Playtime: The Gendering of a Leisure Technology, Comedia*. London; New York: Routledge.

Gray, Mary L. 2009. *Out in the Country: Youth, Media, and Queer Visibility in Rural America*. New York: New York University Press.

Gross, Larry. 2001. *Up from Invisibility: Lesbians, Gay Men and the Media in America*. New York: Columbia University Press.

Hankivsky, Olena, and Daniel Grace. 2015. "Understanding and Emphasizing Difference and Intersectionality in Multimethod and Mixed Methods Research." In *The Oxford Handbook of Multimethod and Mixed Methods Research Inquiry*, edited by S. N. Hesse-Biber and R. B. Johnson, 110–127. Oxford: Oxford University Press.

Hermes, Joke O. K. E. 2014. "Rediscovering Twentieth-Century Feminist Audience Research." In *The Routledge Companion to Media and Gender*, edited by Cindy Carter, Lisa McLaughlin and Linda Steiner, 61–70. New York: Routledge.

Herzog, Herta. 2004. "On Borrowed Experience: An Analysis of Listening to Daytime Sketches." In *Studies in Philosophy and Social Science*, edited by J. D. Peters and P. Simonson, 139–166. Lanham, MD: Rowman and Littlefield.

Hjarvard, Stig. 2013. *The Mediatization of Culture and Society*. New York: Routledge.

Hobson, Dorothy. 1982. *Crossroads: The Drama of a Soap Opera*. Methuen: Limited.

Hochschild, Arlie, and Anne Machung. 2012. *The Second Shift: Working Families and the Revolution at Home*. London: Penguin.

Jacobs, Jerry A., and Kathleen Gerson. 2004. *The Time Divide: Work, Family, and Gender Inequality*. Cambridge, MA: Harvard University Press.

James, E. L. 2012. *Fifty Shades of Grey*. New York: Vintage.

Jenkins, Henry. 2006. *Convergence Culture: Where Old and New Media Collide*. New York: New York University Press.

Jhally, Sut, and Justin Lewis. 1992. *Enlightened Racism: The Cosby Show, Audiences and the Myth of the American Dream*. Boulder, CO: Westview.

Lefebvre, Henri. 1991. *The Critique of Everyday Life, Volume 1*. Translated by John Moore. London: Verso.

Ling, Richard. 2012. *Taken for Grantedness: The Embedding of Mobile Communication in Society*. Cambridge: MIT Press.

Livingstone, Sonia. 2003. "On the Challenges of Cross-National Comparative Media Research." *European Journal of Communication* 18 (4): 477–500.

Livingstone, Sonia. 2013. *Making Sense of Television: The Psychology of Audience Interpretation*. London and New York: Routledge.

Longhurst, Brian. 2007. *Cultural Change and Ordinary Life*. Berkshire: Open University Press, McGraw-Hill.

Lorde, Audre. 1984. *Sister Outisder: Essay and Speeches*. Trumansburg, NY: Crossing Press.

Markham, Annette N. 2013. "Fieldwork in Social Media." *Departures in Critical Qualitative Research* 2 (4): 434–446.

McRobbie, Angela. 1978. "Working Class Girls and the Culture of Femininity." *Women Take Issue: Aspects of Women's Subordination*, 96–108.

Modleski, Tania. 1982. *Loving with a Vengeance: Mass-Produced Fantasies for Women*. Hamden, CT: Archon Books.

Morley, David. 1986. *Family Television: Cultural Power and Domestic Leisure*. London: Comedia.

Muñoz, José Esteban. 1999. *Disidentifications: Queers of Color and the Performance of Politics*. Minneapolis, MN: University of Minnesota Press.

Navar-Gill, Annemarie. Forthcoming. "Tweeting @TheWritersRoom: Hailing the Ideal Fan in Three Writers' Room Twitter Accounts." *Television & New Media*.

Nicholson, Linda J. 1983. "Women, Morality, and History." *Social Research* 50 (3): 514–536.

Nicholson, Linda. 2013. *Feminism/Postmodernism*. London and New York: Routledge.

Parameswaran, Radhika. 2013. "Studying the Elusive Audience: Consumers, Readers, Users, and Viewers in a Changing World." In *The International Encyclopedia of Media Studies Volume IV: Audience and Interpretation*, edited by Radhika Parameswaran, 1–24. Malden MA: Blackwell.

Press, Andrea L. 1990. "Class, Television, and the Female Viewer: Women's Response to *Dynasty*." In *Television and Women's Culture: The Politics of the Popular*, edited by Mary Ellen Brown. Vol. 7: 158–182. Newbury Park, CA: Sage.

Press, Andrea L. 1991. *Women Watching Television: Gender, Class and Generation in the American Television Experience*. Philadelphia, PA: University of Pennsylvania Press.

Press, Andrea L., and Elizabeth R. Cole. 1999. *Speaking of Abortion: Television and Authority in the Lives of Women*. Chicago, IL: University of Chicago Press.

Press, Andrea, and Sonia Livingstone. 2006. "Taking Audience Research into the Age of New Media: Old Problems and New Challenges." In *Questions of Method in Cultural Studies*, edited by M. White and J. Schwoch, 175–200. London: Blackwell.

Press, Andrea L., and Francesca Tripodi. 2014. "Feminism in a Postfeminist World: Who's Hot–And Why We Care–On the Collegiate 'Anonymous Confession Board.'" In *The Routledge Companion to Media and Gender*, edited by C. Carter, L. Steiner, and L. McLaughlin, 543–553. London and New York: Routledge.

Radway, Janice. 1984. *Reading the Romance*. Chapel Hill: University of North Carolina Press.

Reinharz, Shulamit, and Lynn Davidman. 1992. *Feminist Methods in Social Research*. Oxford: Oxford University Press.

Rose, Gillian. 2014. "On the Relation between 'Visual Research Methods' and Contemporary Visual Culture." *The Sociological Review* 62 (1): 24–46.

Scannell, Paddy. 1996. *Radio, Television, and Modern Life: A Phenomenological Approach*, 1996. Oxford: Blackwell Publishing.

Sender, Katherine. 2012. *The Makeover: Reality Television and Reflexive Audiences*. New York: New York University Press.

Shaw, Adrienne. 2015. *Gaming at the Edge: Sexuality and Gender at the Margins of Gamer Culture*. Minneapolis, MN: University of Minnesota Press.

Silverstone, Roger. 1994. *Television and Everyday Life*. London & New York: Routledge.

Skeggs, Beverley, and Helen Wood. 2012. *Reacting to Reality Television: Performance, Audience and Value*. London: Routledge.

Smith, Dorothy. 1987. *The Everyday World as Problematic: A Feminist Sociology*. Boston, MA: Northeastern University Press.

Spigel, Lynn. 1992. *Make Room for TV: Television and the Family Ideal in Postwar America*. Chicago, IL: University of Chicago Press.

Stacey, Judith. 1988. "Can There Be a Feminist Ethnography?" In *Women's Studies International Forum* 11 (1): 21–27.

Taylor, Bryan C., and Thomas R. Lindlof. 2016. "Travelling Methods: Tracing the Globalization of Qualitative Communication Research." *Romanian Journal of Communication and Public Relations* 15 (3): 11–30.

Thiel-Stern, Shayla. 2013. "Beyond the Active Audience." In *The International Encyclopedia of Media Studies*, edited by Angharad N. Valdivia, 389–405. Malden, MA: Wiley-Blackwell.

Turner, Graeme. 2010. *Ordinary People and the Media: The Demotic Turn*. Los Angeles, CA: Sage.

Young, Iris Marion. 1985. "Impartiality and the Civic Public: Some Implications of Feminist Critiques of Moral and Political Theory." *Praxis International* 4: 381–401.

Lemony Liz and likable Leslie: audience understandings of feminism, comedy, and gender in women-led television comedies

Robyn Stacia Swink

ABSTRACT

In this paper, I discuss audience understandings of Tina Fey's *30 Rock*, Amy Poehler's *Parks and Recreation*, Mindy Kaling's *The Mindy Project*, and Lena Dunham's *Girls*. While these women and their shows have been written about and analyzed in the popular press and to a lesser extent in scholarly circles, there is a notable absence of research exploring how audiences understand these shows. Through focus group interviews, I explore audience interpretations of these shows that engage—in some form—with feminist discourses and ideas, paying particular attention to how audience members think these women showrunners impact these shows, and how they see feminism playing a role (or not) in these shows. I argue that while these audience members enjoyed the shows, ambivalence permeated their understanding of and relationship to the shows, not only in their perceptions of the shows as feminist, but also resulting from their interpretation of the humor and gender dynamics of the shows. Ultimately, the audience members' conflicted interpretations of the shows reflect larger trends in the post-feminist media environment. Further, their readings of the shows point to the potential limits of feminist humor for post-feminist audience members.

Introduction: television comedies and feminism

You know my code: hoes before bros. Uteruses before duderuses. Ovaries before brovaries. (Leslie Knope, *Parks and Recreation*)

I pretty much just do whatever Oprah tells me to. (Liz Lemon, *30 Rock*)

Leslie Knope's pro-woman credo and Liz Lemon's love of Oprah are well-known among viewers of *Parks and Recreation* and *30 Rock*. What is less well-known is how viewers interpret characters like these, their shows, and their sometimes ambiguous yet comedic engagement with both feminist and "faux" feminist discourses. To better understand the ways that audiences make sense of gender, feminism, and comedy in a post-feminist media environment, I interviewed regular watchers of four popular shows with women who work both as showrunners and stars on the shows: Tina Fey's *30 Rock* (NBC 2006–2013), Amy Poehler's *Parks and Recreation* (NBC 2009–2015), Mindy Kaling's *The Mindy Project* (FOX/HULU 2012–present), and Lena Dunham's *Girls* (HBO 2012–present).

In addition to being recognized for their successes with their various cultural products, Tina Fey, Amy Poehler, Mindy Kaling, and Lena Dunham are often considered as a cohort by the popular press (see Daniel D'Addario 2014; Peter Gicas 2013; Ray Richmond 2013). Further, these women are frequently discussed in relation to their own versions of feminism, or lack of this (for examples see: Kaitlin Ebersol 2015; Deanne Kaczerski 2014; Katie Roiphe 2011; Valentina Valentini 2015; Jazmine Woodberry 2013). Given the current post-feminist media environment, it is notable that these women and their shows become a vehicle for conversations about feminism. A central goal of this project is to understand what this conversation entails for viewers of these shows. Some of the larger research questions guiding the project include: what is the relationship between feminism and comedy in audience interpretation of comedic texts? How is gender implicated in audience identification and enjoyment of potentially feminist comedy shows? How are feminist humor and comedic representations of feminism interpreted by audiences in a post-feminist media environment?

I found that while these audience members enjoy the shows for various reasons, ambivalence permeated their understanding of and relationship to the shows; not only in their perceptions of the shows as feminist, but also resulting from their interpretation of the humor and gender dynamics of the shows. Ultimately, the audience members' conflicted interpretations of the shows reflect larger trends in the post-feminist media environment. Additionally, their readings of the shows point to the potential limits of feminist humor for post-feminist audience members.

The shows

To provide some background on the television shows that I investigate, *30 Rock* is a satire that focuses on Liz Lemon (Tina Fey), the head writer of a sketch comedy show. *30 Rock* follows Liz's work life, focusing on her relationship with her boss and mentor, Jack Donaghy (Alec Baldwin), and her attempts to manage the stars of her show, Tracy Jordan (Tracy Morgan) and Jenna Maroney (Jane Krakowski). A central theme in *30 Rock* includes Liz's attempts and failures at having both a successful professional and personal life, with her work often dominating her life and getting in the way of romances and friendships. *30 Rock* was created by Tina Fey; Fey also writes for, executive produces and stars in the show.

Parks and Recreation centers on Leslie Knope (Amy Poehler) who works in the Parks and Recreation department in the fictional Pawnee, Indiana. *Parks and Recreation* is shot in the "mockumentary" style which includes frequent scenes with characters speaking directly to the camera. The show follows Leslie's workplace relationships including with her boss Ron Swanson (Nick Offerman) and her best friend Ann Perkins (Rashida Jones) among others. Leslie is portrayed as a "go-getter" who is deeply committed to both her professional and personal relationships. The show follows Leslie's career advancement and romantic developments, including her marriage to Ben Wyatt (Adam Scott). Amy Poehler produces and stars in *Parks and Recreation*; Poehler also wrote six episodes and directed three episodes of the show.

Since the participants discussed *The Mindy Project* and *Girls* significantly less than the other two shows, I will be briefer in describing them. *The Mindy Project* stars Mindy Kaling as an obstetrician-gynecologist, Mindy Lahiri. While the show is often set in the workplace, it focuses more on Lahiri's personal life than on her life as a successful doctor. *The Mindy Project* was created by Mindy Kaling; Kaling also writes for, executive produces and stars in the show.

Girls follows the life of Hannah Horvath (Lena Dunham), a twenty-something who recently graduated college and is trying to find her place in life while living in New York City. The show also follows three of her female friends who struggle with their romantic relationships and their attempts to find stable jobs. *Girls* was created by Lena Dunham; Dunham also writes for, executive produces, directs (fifteen episodes out of forty-two), and stars in the show. While these shows differ in content and style, they are all woman-led and feature a central female character comically navigating her daily life.

(Post-)feminism, comedy, and media

These shows exist in a so-called "post-feminist" era which not only frames the content of shows, but also situates the audience members. There are differing perspectives on what constitutes post-feminism. Rosalind Gill (2008, 442) refers to the "post-feminist sensibility" which is a response to feminism, but is particularly complex "because of its tendency to entangle feminist and antifeminist discourses." Angela McRobbie (2009, 130) argues that the post-feminist landscape depends on acknowledging feminism in the first place: "I define post-feminism as a kind of anti-feminism, which is reliant, paradoxically, on an assumption that feminism has been taken into account." In this sense, McRobbie suggests that while post-feminism is predicated on the sense that "we don't need feminism anymore," feminism continues to haunt the landscape. Most scholars agree that post-feminism is characterized by a focus on individual empowerment rather than group concerns, which is bolstered and fostered through consumer culture. Furthermore, privilege and a re-centering of middle-class whiteness are central to the post-feminist landscape. McRobbie (2009, 41) refers to this as "nostalgia for whiteness." Diane Negra (2009, 153) summarizes the issue: "In tracking the characteristic preoccupations of post-feminism, what is perhaps most striking is the diversity of identities and social experiences it neglects." This lack of and insensitivity to diversity is a common critique of these four shows and the potentially homogenous audiences they appeal to.

Certain texts have received considerable attention as emblematic of post-feminism, including *Sex and the City*, *Ally McBeal*, and the Bridget Jones films (see Jane Gerhard 2005; Amanda D. Lotz 2001; Angela McRobbie 2004, 2008; Rachel Moseley and Jacinda Read 2002). The differing perspectives on the potential feminism of the four shows at the center of this project indicate that the ambiguous post-feminist sensibility persists. However, these shows do not seem to embrace the choice-centered, consumption driven, and "femininity alongside feminism" version of post-feminism that is evident in *Sex and the City* and *Ally McBeal*. Instead these shows seem to be more critical in their engagement with feminist discourses. For this project though I am centrally interested in understanding how *audiences* are interpreting the content of the contemporary representations of feminism in these shows.

Given the ambiguity surrounding feminism's place in popular culture, viewers' interpretations of comedic (potentially) feminist shows are important to examine since humor often straddles incongruities and embraces ambiguities (Jeroen Vandaele 2002). Likewise, when engaging in reception studies of comedy shows, it is imperative to remember the inherently polysemic nature of humor (Jerry Palmer 1987). Comedic texts are particularly ambiguous and open to interpretation because humor is frequently predicated on disrupting expectations or playing with conceptual inconsistencies, leading to *dramatically* different interpretations of the humorous content (Murray S. Davis 1993). Dave Chappelle famously left his popular *Comedy Central* show over this precise concern; he was uncertain if audiences were interpreting his comedy to bolster racist perspectives or to undermine them (Raúl Pérez 2013). Because a critical reading of the texts alone offers inadequate data on the complex interactions among the contested status of feminism and the polysemic potentials of comedy, I conducted an analysis of audiences' responses to these four shows.

Feminist and post-feminist humor

When talking about "women's comedy/humor," there is often a slippage between "women's humor" and "feminist humor" (Joanne R. Gilbert 2004). The most basic definition of "women's humor" is humor produced by and/or for women. There are varying definitions of feminist humor, but upon their review of the literature, Limor Shifman and Dafna Lemish (2011, 255) identify several basic characteristics related to feminist humor:

> [F]irst, feminist humor is oppositional, as it criticizes the current state of gender inequalities and hegemonic stereotyping. Second, as an expression of empowerment, feminist humor relates to the capability for empowerment and freedom to express critical thoughts. Consequentially, feminist humor often refers to the ability to create humor that mocks men and hegemonic masculinity. Finally, feminist humor requires access to an outlet that is a "stage" or a medium, through which this kind of humor is expressed and spread.

Additionally, scholars suggest that humor and comedy are uniquely qualified means for engaging with feminist ideas and sentiments. For example, Frances Gray (1994) argues that because of the male dominance in comedy, it is an especially important place for feminist critics to step in and "break silences" about gender politics. Linda Mizejewski (2014, 6) also recognizes the important relationship between women's comedy and feminism in contemporary media, arguing that "women's comedy has become a primary site in mainstream pop culture where feminism speaks, talks back, and is contested." While there is certainly potential for feminist humor to disrupt the gender regime, it is also important to consider the role and nature of *post-feminist* humor.

The post-feminist sensibility is characterized by irony and play. For example, Rosalind Gill (2007, 159) writes that "in post-feminist media culture irony has become a way of 'having it both ways,' of expressing sexist or homophobic or otherwise unpalatable sentiments in a ironized form, while claiming this was not actually 'meant.'" This ironic stance reflects the inherent ambiguity in the post-feminist sensibility. Similarly, Karrin Vasby Anderson and Kristina Horn Sheeler (2014, 227) point to the ways that post-feminism often manifests as a playful alternative to the seemingly "intractable and dour" depictions of feminism. While Limor Shifman and Dafna Lemish (2010, 6) are hesitant to define post-feminist humor since it is understudied, they suggest a few defining characteristics: first, while post-feminist humor does not emphasize the gendered hierarchy, post-feminist humor focuses on gender differences; because of this focus on difference, post-feminist humor targets both men and women; "the context of post-feminist humor is the world of leisure and consumption rather than politics or work"; and post-feminist humor emphasizes women as sexually empowered and "proactive."

In considering the four shows central to this project, it seems that both feminist humor and post-feminist humor are evident in varying degrees in each of the shows. However, the inherently polysemic nature of humor means audiences can interpret the same content in very different ways; therefore understanding the *audience* members' interpretations is the focus of this project. While there are numerous popular press articles as well as some scholarly work written about the relationship between these women, their shows and comedy, there is an absence of work exploring how audiences are making sense of these shows. This project is an important first step in filling this gap.

The study

In order to explore audiences' understanding of women-run television comedies, I conducted three focus group interviews with students at a Midwestern university. There were a total of twenty participants, with interviews lasting between sixty and ninety minutes. While focus groups cannot offer a transparent view of everyday talk, they more closely approximate this than the one-on-one research interview (Peter Lunt and Sonia Livingstone 1996).

I posted recruitment flyers throughout the college campus and in coffee shops in the community. I also used my social networks on campus to recruit participants. The recruitment flyers asked, "Do you regularly watch shows like *30 Rock*, *Parks and Recreation*, *The Mindy Project* or *Girls?* You are invited to participate in a research study about audience responses to television comedies written, directed, and/or produced by women." While this open ended script allowed participants to classify themselves as regular watchers of the shows, it also most likely primed them for a discussion about women and gender in television.

I conducted the interviews during the spring and fall of 2015. The participants completed a brief survey before we began the group interviews. The survey included demographic items as well as basic questions about which shows they watched, what their favorite shows were, and whether or not they identified themselves as feminists.

Based on their survey responses, the majority of the participants identified themselves as white, heterosexual women. There were sixteen women and four men, and fifteen participants identified as white, one identified as black, one identified as Hispanic/Latina, one identified as South Asian, one identified as Asian, and one identified as both Asian and white. Fifteen respondents identified themselves as feminists, while five did not. Twelve of the participants were either in graduate school at the time of the interview or had some graduate school education, while eight of the participants were undergraduate students. The participants ranged in age from eighteen to thirty-four years old, with an average age of twenty-four.

The demographics of this group of participants impacted the interview responses in a few ways. First, given the relatively high levels of education among the participants and the fact that most of them self-identified as feminists, several of them spoke with relative competence regarding gender and feminism. In addition, the majority of the participants were white. Considering that the post-feminist milieu is characterized by a re-centering of whiteness, it is possible that these shows resonated with white viewers more profoundly than with viewers of color. Further, white viewers may more easily identify with central characters when they are also white. While it is important to consider my findings in light of this particularly privileged demographic of participants, it also seems likely that these shows are appealing to this demographic more than others.

In the pre-interview survey, participants indicated which shows they watched "regularly": seventeen participants watched *Parks and Recreation*, thirteen participants watched *30 Rock*, six participants watched *Girls*, while only three participants watched *The Mindy Project*. While the participants discussed all four shows to some degree, their discussion largely focused on *30 Rock* and *Parks and Recreation*.

Two of the focus groups included seven participants, and one group included six participants. While all of the participants did not know one another, in every group there were some participants who knew each other from previous coursework or other school-related networks. Fortunately, in each group this familiarity among some participants seemed to facilitate a more comfortable atmosphere for the entire group. I began the discussion with general questions about the shows and then asked more specific questions about the characters, the humor in the shows, the potential feminism of the shows, and the women who run and star in the shows. See the Appendix for the interview guide.

Ambivalent enjoyment, conflicted identification

While the focus group participants enjoyed these shows, they were also ambivalent about them in many ways. First, several participants described these shows as the best available options in the current television landscape. Additionally, several participants identified strongly with some of the central women characters on the shows, yet this identification was often unfavorable.

The participants' enjoyment of the shows was palpable throughout the interviews. For example, Ruby[1] was expressive about her love for *Parks and Recreation*, and she explained that she even ended the celebration of her husband's birthday early so they could come home and watch the series finale. Another poignant example of a participant's passion and enjoyment of the shows was in Phoebe's comments about *30 Rock*: "I fall asleep to an episode of *30 Rock* every night"; "I literally can quote every episode of *30 Rock*, like I'm concerned"; "Now that I'm in this [residential] hall, I'll put on Netflix in the shower and have [*30 Rock*] on"; and "*30 Rock* is my own thing, it's a relationship I'm in." While Phoebe framed her relationship to *30 Rock* as mildly compulsive, her enjoyment of the show was extremely evident. She was one of many of the participants who expressed strong attachments to the shows.

While participants expressed affinity for these shows, they also expressed some ambivalence about them, specifically referring to them as "good enough" when compared to other shows. For example, when comparing the gender depictions on these shows to others, Gloria said, "So when you do see something like *The Mindy Project* or *Parks and Recreation*, it's like 'Oh god! Finally!' It's a little more progressive or real." Gloria's exclamation clearly indicated a sense of relief that these shows have emerged on television at last. This relief stemmed from the "realness" of the shows rather than being stereotypical (i.e., *not* progressive). Ruby also mentioned that these shows are better than other options, even though their gender politics are fallible:

> As feminist as I want to say Amy Poehler/Leslie Knope and that show [*Parks and Recreation*] is, there are obviously some things that were not [feminist]. And because of what our choices are a lot of times, I'll look at it and I'm like "Good enough!" I'll take it, and I'll run with it. And the same thing with Lena Dunham. Like there's so much shit in that show that it just makes me cringe. And they are catty and not supportive of one another and they're awful, but then there's other things. It's like "Oh Lena! You look like me! Thank god, 'cause nobody else on TV does." And Mindy too.

While Ruby expressed her extreme fondness for some of the shows elsewhere in the interview, she suggested that this affinity is tempered and emerges from relatively low expectations given the other programs that are available. Notably, both Gloria and Ruby situated their comments about the shows in somewhat political terms like "more progressive" and "as a feminist," pointing to the tension between their desire for television that reflects their world views and the reality of what is actually available to watch. Their comments highlight the fact that, when it comes to representations of gender and feminism, there is limited content available in the post-feminist media environment.

This limited representation was reflected not only in participants' comments about the *shows*, but was also evident in their conflicted identification with the kinds of women *characters* on the shows. First, several participants strongly identified with some of the characters and got pleasure from this identification. Clara best exemplified this when she said "I feel like Tina Fey/Liz Lemon is my spirit animal. I relate so much to the character of Liz Lemon. I love her." While participants could identify with some of the characters, this identification was often unflattering. For example, Ruby said,

> If I had to identify with anybody in that show I mean it has to be Liz Lemon because there are certainly parts of me that are awkward and weird and I don't know how to act right in public .... I guess that would have to be Liz, for sure.

So while Ruby admitted that she identifies with Liz, it's not because she identifies with admirable traits. Rather she identifies with more of Liz's "flaws." Mildred echoed this sentiment, "I feel like I kind of identify with Liz Lemon in the sense of she's awkward and doesn't know how to deal perfectly with the situations that she finds herself in." Like Ruby, Mildred notes identifying with Liz's "awkwardness."

Notably, this tempered identification only happened with the more failure-prone characters like Liz Lemon, Mindy Lahiri, and the characters on *Girls*, whereas identification with the high-achieving Leslie Knope was more positive. Virginia captured this contrast in identification when she said, "I see my enthusiasm and attachment to other people in Leslie Knope, and I see my hypocrisy and not having it together-ness in Mindy." So while Virginia identified with both Leslie and Mindy, what she related to with Leslie are more conventionally positive attributes, whereas her identification with Mindy is distinctly less favorable. In a sense, this ambivalent identification with failure-prone characters is not surprising: humans are flawed and can recognize similar flaws in some of their oft-watched characters. However, the fact that this conflicted identification happened with the more fallible, yet comical characters suggests that there may be limits to the comedic gendered commentary of these characters. I will discuss this further in an upcoming section.

Gender, feminism, and comedy

When participants discussed their favorite characters and the characters that they identify with, a telling gender dynamic emerged. While several participants *identified* strongly with female characters, they often claimed that their *favorite* characters were men. For example, in response to the question "Which character do you identify with on *30 Rock*?" Clara said,

> Liz Lemon. I find myself saying things that she says. I definitely identify with her. I also like her, I empathize with her. But if I had to pick favorite characters on that show, I think it would have to be Jack Donaghy.

Similarly, Ruby identified with *30 Rock*'s Liz Lemon (discussed above) while favoring Kenneth: "My favorite is Kenneth. He's just funny." Further, when discussing *Parks and Recreation*, Ruby noted that her favorites on the show include Jean-Ralphio, and that some of the funniest moments of the show feature the character Andy Dwyer.

This pattern of identifying with women but favoring men for their humor is notable given the persistent stereotype that women are not as funny as men (Gilbert 2004; Gray 1994). While these four women are challenging this stereotype by running popular comedic shows, the participants did not see them as favorites for their comedic skills, even though they identify with them for other reasons. This suggests that these women characters may still be read in relation to this humorless stereotype. Interestingly, these women often contribute to writing the content for the male characters, suggesting that their ideas are considered the "funniest" even if their own performances are not. Inger-Lise Kalviknes Bore (2010) had a similar finding in her study of sketch comedy shows: even when women identified with the "female" themes of the shows, they didn't necessarily perceive the shows as funny, indicating that identification is distinct from being comically entertained.

In addition to favoring male characters for being funny, some participants favored male characters for being the "most feminist" characters on the shows. For example, in discussing her favorite *30 Rock* character, Jack Donaghy, Clara says

> I think the most feminist character on *30 Rock* is Jack Donaghy. I really do. I realize he's supposed to be the embodiment of hegemonic masculinity, but think about his character. He chooses Liz Lemon of all people to be his protégé; he treats her with respect; he treats all the dates, even Condoleezza Rice, with respect; ... [his wife] is kidnapped in North Korea and he raises their child.

In response to Clara's comment, Alice discusses one of her favorite characters on *Parks and Recreation*: "I usually think Ron Swanson is the most feminist character on *Parks and Rec* too. We were talking about the hegemonic masculinity—like total example of that. But he never views things in terms of gender." This finding is notable because one of the appeals of the shows for these participants is the more "progressive" gender dynamics, yet they are claiming that male characters are more—rather than *as*—feminist than the female characters. In part, this suggests that viewers might expect the central female characters to be feminist, but not expect the same from powerful male characters and are thus surprised to see such feminist traits in the men. More broadly, this gendered tension between identification and favorites indicates that the potentially feminist humor of both male and female characters is encountered in ambiguous ways by audiences reflecting ongoing contradictions of the post-feminist media environment.

The participants also expressed ambivalence and uncertainty about the overall role of feminism in the shows. Additionally, their perceptions of the feminist messages in the shows were influenced by their impressions of the women behind the shows. In response to my question about the potential feminism in the show, Mildred said,

> I don't really think [*30 Rock*] is a feminist show. I mean, I feel like themes of feminism come up because the central character is a woman and she does things that we don't expect to see a woman do on TV, but I wouldn't say its main goal is to be about feminism.

In this response, Mildred notably associated "themes of feminism" with the mere fact that Liz Lemon is a woman, but then argued that the larger goals of the show are not necessarily feminist. Mildred's (and others') responses get at a common confusion and conflation between perceiving the shows as feminist and seeing the characters as feminist. Kathryn Kein (2015, 678) discusses this tendency to look at Liz Lemon for the "thesis statement" of the show, thus overlooking or misinterpreting how the show is feminist in a broader sense. Another example of this confusion was in Irene's response to the same question about feminism in the shows. Referring to the characters on *Girls*, Irene said, "I think the characters kind of engage with feminism, but I don't know if they *are* feminist. Does that make sense?" So while I ask the group if they see the *shows* as feminist, Irene and others respond with whether or not they see the *characters* as feminist. This uncertainty about the characters being feminist is contributing to the general trouble with unequivocally calling the shows "feminist television shows."

Several other participants articulated the difficulty with calling the shows wholly feminist. For example, Alice initially said that she sees the shows as feminist, but then hedged her statement:

> It's a tough question … I would say yes because … [the shows are] pointing out a lot of stuff and a lot of inequality and just like problems, and I think that's a good. I mean … it's good enough, like that's a good start … Not everybody has to have the feminist flag waving in order for it to be beneficial for women, for us to relate to it … but I do think they are trying to make a point. And I think the feminist kind of point would be one that they're going for, for sure.

Similar to previous statements about the shows being "good enough" in comparison to other television shows, Alice made the point that these shows are "good enough" or a "good start" when it comes to gender politics and feminism. However, Alice then qualified her statement by suggesting that the shows do not have to have a "feminist flag waving," implying that there is a difference between being overt with feminist messages versus more subtle attempts to insert messages about gender inequality into the shows.

Other participants talked explicitly about the idea of a "feminist agenda" in the show. Ruby said "I don't think they can come in with a feminist agenda in the beginning." Alice agreed with Ruby and added, "A feminist agenda would probably have killed the shows." In suggesting that an overt feminist message would be harmful to the shows' success, Ruby and Alice both demonstrated an awareness of the popular stigma associated with feminism, yet they also suggested that an overt "feminist agenda" is not necessary to make points about gender inequality. Their comments also seem to reflect McRobbie's (2009, 55) understanding of post-feminism: "The various political issues associated with feminism are understood to be now widely recognized and responded to (they have become feminist common sense) with the effect that there is no longer a place for feminism in contemporary political culture." The conflict with definitively calling the shows feminist, yet still seeing elements of feminism in the shows is emblematic of this post-feminist landscape that simultaneously entangles elements of feminism with an aversion towards feminism.

Furthermore, a few participants pointed out the media's tendency to "brand" the television shows in a particular way when they are women-led. Lillian said:

> I do feel like these shows are being identified as feminist television. I feel like because they give that label to like every show written by a woman it kind of, really loses—it doesn't necessarily go with that. I feel like they do address issues of gender, but I can't necessarily say "Yes, this show is a feminist television show."

Lillian was aware of the problems with collapsing the category woman with the category feminism and pointed out the difference between addressing gender and being a feminist television show. Lillian's comments exemplify the difficulty of definitively identifying feminism for post-feminist audiences. Moreover, her comment about the "label" of feminism being applied points to a common feature of post-feminism in which a kind of faux-feminism is co-opted in service of a consumer and market-driven society.

The participants' difficulty with classifying these shows as feminist is most likely related to the fact that several participants identify themselves as feminists, and even have some graduate training in feminist theory and are thus aware of all the complexities of calling something feminist. And even if that's not the case, it is clear that their affinity for the shows was laden with ambivalence: they saw the shows as doing *something* with gender and feminism, yet not necessarily demonstrating explicit and overt feminist politics.

The participants' perceptions of the shows as feminist or not were also impacted by their general perceptions of the women behind the shows. Part of these perceptions came from the participants reading the semi-auto-biographical books written by the women: Tina Fey's *Bossypants* (2011), Amy Poehler's *Yes Please* (2014), Mindy Kaling's *Is Everyone Hanging Out Without Me (and other Concerns)* (2012), and Lena Dunham's *Not That Kind of Girl* (2014). Not only do the books provide insight into the larger perspectives of the women, but the participants, with their frequent mentions of the books, indicated that they use them as paratexts to understand the goals behind the women's creative work and careers (Jonathan Gray 2010). A good example of this is when Gloria spoke broadly about the women's "projects" and specifically Amy Poehler's work with *Smart Girls* (an organization created by Poehler and Meredith Walker "dedicated to helping young people cultivate their authentic selves" [amysmartgirls.com] 2016):

> I feel like it becomes a passion project that is part of this group of projects they do. Like when Amy Poehler—I don't know when she started to do the Smart Girls thing on social media. So I feel like you saw that start to inform the show a little bit. And they all have books; it tells you something that it's not just the show in isolation. It's part of this kind of overall, I say ideology. That's probably not the right word, but it goes through all of these things—it's bigger than that. And you kind of see how when they're running it; it crosses over into lots of different places. It's bigger than a show I think.

Thelma echoed Gloria's point in discussing the potential feminism of the shows as well as seeing the shows as extensions of the women:

> I sort of have a problem with comparing them as feminist or not feminist.... These are women who are participating in writing these shows who I believe self-identify as feminists. And so if we're looking at their motivation, like their motivation behind this piece of art, wouldn't everything that they do be part of their feminist extension of themselves?

Even though Thelma was reluctant to make claims about the shows as feminist or not feminist, she saw these shows as inevitably feminist *to an extent* since she considers the women behind the shows feminist. Clearly the participants were reading the shows in part through their perceptions of the feminist politics of the women behind them, most likely impacting their interpretation of the comedy in the shows and the characters that these women portray.

Politics, feelings, and (post-)feminist representations

The participants frequently noted their feelings about the perceived tone of the characters and shows. This was particularly evident with *30 Rock* and *Parks and Recreation*. There was a trend among the participants to more willingly embrace the "positivity" of Leslie Knope and *Parks and Recreation* and express more conflict regarding Liz Lemon and *30 Rock*.

Sometimes this positivity was connected to Leslie Knope, and other times participants discussed an overall upbeat tone to the show. For example, in discussing the finale of *Parks and Recreation*, Gloria said, "You felt good at the end … and so I was happy with it." Similarly, Hazel said, "It was very good tonally. Because *Parks and Rec* has always been a feel good show. They didn't change that." Ruby describes Leslie Knope as

> this bad ass and everybody is so supportive of her and is always team Leslie. She's such a good friend, and then she gets to have this romantic success. And it's just so optimistic, and I think that's why I have more favorable feelings about it.

Gloria echoes the sentiment about Leslie Knope: "I would love to hang out with Leslie Knope. And I wouldn't mind being more like her, it's aspirational."

The allure of the positive tone of *Parks and Recreation* and Leslie Knope was contrasted by conflicted feelings about the more failure-prone characters, including Liz Lemon. For example, Ruby said,

> [Liz Lemon and Mindy Kaling] have a very similar kind of hapless world … Liz Lemon is just kind of this sad sack. I get that it's sort of the feminist, career thing behind her. But it's all that like "you can be very successful at your job, but you're still just a personal shit show."

Virginia extended this sentiment:

> I feel like Tina Fey among many of the comedy writers is one of the least likable. I loved her at first, and then I think later on, as *Parks and Recreation* became more popular, I felt like Leslie Knope was just a lot more likable and like Liz Lemon had this sort of this sour quality to her.

(See Eleanor Patterson 2012 for a discussion of the common slippage between this character and actress.) Instead of identifying this "haplessness" as a humorous feminist commentary on the gendered expectations for women, several participants simply find the portrayals not as appealing, especially in contrast to the more traditionally "successful" Leslie Knope. It seems that regardless of the participants' awareness of the potential feminism of the shows, the comedic portrayals that leave them feeling "good" resonate with them more than the comedic portrayals that are more discouraging or pessimistic.

This seems to stem in part from the way that feminism is represented in the shows. According to Mizejewski (2014) *30 Rock* satirizes femininity, post-feminism, and certain versions of feminism. Liz Lemon can be read as a satire of more privileged versions of feminism, and post-feminism is satirized through the tension between Jenna and Liz because Jenna's obsession with femininity is often placed in humorous contrast to Liz's brand of feminism (Mizejewski 2014). Liz's failure-prone nature can also be read as critiquing the ridiculous expectations for femininity (for example, consider an instance where Liz is trying to seduce a man and calls for "double, no triple Spanx"). While there are many elements of feminist humor in *30 Rock*, the show ultimately ends with Liz Lemon getting married, adopting children, and returning to work: reflecting a characteristically post-feminist focus on finding an *individual* balance between romance, work, and family life.

In contrast to the failure-prone Liz Lemon, Leslie Knope is consistently portrayed as a "go-getter" who doesn't get easily deterred by obstacles, and she continues to achieve success in both her personal and professional life. While Leslie is frequently explicit about being a feminist and emphasizes the importance of supporting women, the show features a version of the post-feminist focus on empowerment and "girl power" which can work to playfully eclipse the drudgery associated with feminist social justice work (Anderson and Sheeler 2014; Shifman and Lemish 2011). Clearly both characters and shows are entangling feminist and post-feminist discourses in a variety of subtle ways. While the participants seem to be in tune with this to an extent, they also seem to prefer the more "empowering" representations of feminism found in Leslie Knope. The participants' conflicting relationships to the two characters seem to point to the ambiguity inherent in post-feminist media objects, as well as suggesting the limits to potentially feminist comedy in a post-feminist media environment.

Conclusion

This study examined audience perspectives on the following popular women-run television comedies: Tina Fey's *30 Rock*, Amy Poehler's *Parks and Recreation*, Mindy Kaling's *The Mindy Project*, and Lena Dunham's *Girls*. While these women and their shows have been written about elsewhere, there is no scholarly work exploring how *audiences* are making sense of these shows. Given the particularly polysemic nature of humor, critical textual readings of the shows are insufficient when it comes to understanding the ways that the content and humor in the shows is interpreted by audiences. Overall, I was particularly surprised to learn about the *feelings* that undergirded the participants' perceptions of both the characters and the shows, and focus groups were a good method to elicit these sentiments. Another revealing benefit of using focus groups was learning which shows the participants gravitated towards among the four initially proposed: they favored and centrally discussed *30 Rock* and *Parks and Recreation*. The lack of discussion around *Girls* could be related to class and economics: it is on HBO, a premium network and thus more expensive to access. It was notable that *The Mindy Project* was not as widely discussed considering that she is the only woman of color featured centrally in these four shows. This potentially reflects the dominance of whiteness both in post-feminist media objects and for post-feminist media audiences (McRobbie 2009; Negra 2009).

This project takes an important step in exploring how audiences interpret the potential feminism of these shows and to broadly understand the connections between gender, feminism, and comedy for audiences. I found that these participants expressed a great deal of ambivalence concerning these shows: they see the shows as the best available options given the current television landscape, and while they identified strongly with some of the characters on the shows this identification was often fraught with tension. Additionally, while the participants identified with women characters, they often favored male characters both for their comedic abilities and their feminism. The participants were also conflicted concerning the role of feminism in the shows, with their previous knowledge of the women behind the shows impacting their perceptions. Notably, the participants gravitated towards the more positive and traditionally successful Leslie Knope while expressing dissatisfaction with the more failure-prone Liz Lemon. While both characters entangle feminist and post-feminist characteristics, Leslie Knope seemingly appeals to the empowerment and "girl power" narratives characteristic of post-feminism. The fact that the more post-feminist representation of a woman appeals to the participants more than the comedic feminist commentary central to Liz Lemon, suggests that there may be limited potentials for feminist humor in a post-feminist media environment. This pattern may also speak to the limits of using feminist humor specifically in a situation comedy. For example, Patricia Mellencamp (1986) argues that the subversive potential of comedy can ultimately be trumped by the generic constraints of the narrative in sit-coms. In this sense, feminist humor may be more successfully disruptive in other genres, including stand-up.

All of these findings point to the ambiguous media environment of post-feminism: not only are the shows reflective of post-feminist sentiments, but the audience members are also embedded in a post-feminist media environment. While it is not clear that feminist humor can flourish in this post-feminist environment, at least these viewers were not passively encountering the potentially feminist messages in these shows. Instead, these viewers actively struggled to clarify their responses to and understanding of the contradictions in comedic and entertaining representations of (post-)feminism.

Note

1.   Each participant was given a pseudonym.

Acknowledgement

The research was conducted with the approval of the Institutional Review Board of the University of Missouri, Columbia.

Disclosure statement

No potential conflict of interest was reported by the author.

References

30 Rock. 2006–2013. Television Series. 1-7. USA: NBC.
Ally McBeal. 1997–2002. Television Series. Seasons 1–5. USA: Fox.
"Amy Poehler's Smart Girls". 2016. http://amysmartgirls.com/
Anderson, Karrin Vasby, and Kristina Horn Sheeler. 2014. "Texts (and Tweets) from HIllary: Meta-Meming and Postfeminist Political Culture." *Presidential Studies Quarterly* 44 (2): 224–243.
Bore, Inger-Lise Kalviknes. 2010. "(Un)funny Women: TV comedy Audiences and the Gendering of Humour." *European Journal of Cultural Studies* 13 (2): 139–154.
D'Addario, Daniel. 2014. "Tina Fey and Amy Poehler: Hollywood's Imperfect Feminists." http://www.salon.com/2014/01/12/tina_fey_and_amy_poehler_hollywoods_imperfect_feminists/
Davis, Murray S. 1993. *What's so Funny?: The Comic Conception of Culture and Society*. Chicago, IL: University of Chicago Press.
Dunham, Lena. 2014. *Not That Kind of Girl: A Young Woman Tells You What She's "Learned"*. New York, NY: Random House.
Ebersol, Kaitlin. 2015. "Lena Dunham, Amy Poehler and the Modern Feminist Discourse." *High Brow Magazine*.   http://www.highbrowmagazine.com/4588-lena-dunham-amy-poehler-and-modern-feminist-discourse
Fey, Tina. 2011. *Bossypants*. New York, NY: Reagan Arthur / Little, Brown.
Gerhard, Jane. 2005. "Sex and the City." *Feminist Media Studies* 5 (1): 37–49.
Gicas, Peter. 2013. "Lena Dunham Watches Tina Fey's Girls Parody." *E! Online*. http://www.eonline.com/news/464728/lena-dunham-watches-tina-fey-s-girls-parody-on-saturday-night-live-at-mindy-kaling-s-house-see-the-pic

FEMINIST RECEPTION STUDIES IN A POST-AUDIENCE AGE

Gilbert, Joanne R. 2004. *Performing Marginality: Humor, Gender, and Cultural Critique*. Detroit, MI: Wayne State University Press.

Gill, Rosalind. 2007. "Postfeminist Media Culture: Elements of a Sensibility." *European Journal of Cultural Studies* 10 (2): 147–166.

Gill, Rosalind. 2008. "Culture and Subjectivity in Neoliberal and Postfeminist Times." *Subjectivity* 25 (1): 432–445.

Girls. 2012–present. Television Series. Seasons 1-5. USA: HBO.

Gray, Frances. 1994. *Women and Laughter*. Charlottesville: University of Virginia Press.

Gray, Jonathan. 2010. *Show Sold Separately: Promos, Spoilers, and Other Media Paratexts*. New York, NY: New York University Press.

Kaczerski, Deanne. 2014. "Mindy Kaling: The Accidental New Voice of Feminism." *Marie Claire*. http://www.marieclaire.com/celebrity-lifestyle/mindy-kaling-sxsw-2014

Kaling, Mindy. 2012. *Is Everyone Hanging Out Without Me?*. New York, NY: Three Rivers Press.

Kein, Kathryn. 2015. "Recovering Our Sense of Humor: New Directions in Feminist Humor Studies." *Feminist Studies* 41 (3): 671–681.

Lotz, Amanda D. 2001. "Postfeminist Television Criticism: Rehabilitating Critical Terms and Identifying Postfeminist Attributes." *Feminist Media Studies* 1 (1): 105–121.

Lunt, Peter, and Sonia Livingstone. 1996. "Rethinking the Focus Group in Media and Communications Research." *Journal of Communication* 46 (2): 79–98.

McRobbie, Angela. 2004. "Post-feminism and Popular Culture." *Feminist Media Studies* 4 (3): 255–264.

McRobbie, Angela. 2008. "Young Women and Consumer Culture." *Cultural Studies* 22 (5): 531–550.

McRobbie, Angela. 2009. *The Aftermath of Feminism*. London: Sage.

Mellencamp, Patricia. 1986. "Situation Comedy, Feminism and Freud: Discourses of Gracie and Lucy." In *Studies in Entertainment: Critical Approaches to Mass Culture*, edited by T. Modleski, 88–95. Bloomington: Indiana University Press.

Mizejewski, Linda. 2014. *Pretty/Funny Women Comedians and Body Politics*. Austin: University of Texas Press.

Moseley, Rachel, and Jacinda Read. 2002. "'Having It Ally': Popular Television (Post-) Feminism." *Feminist Media Studies* 2 (2): 231–249.

Negra, Diane. 2009. *What a Girl Wants?: Fantasizing the Reclamation of Self in Postfeminism*. New York, NY: Routledge.

Palmer, Jerry. 1987. *The Logic of the Absurd: On Film and Television Comedy*. London: BFI.

Parks and Recreation. 2009–2015. Television Series. Seasons 1–7. USA: NBC.

Patterson, Eleanor. 2012. "Fracturing Tina Fey: A Critical Analysis of Postfeminist Television Comedy Stardom." *The Communication Review* 15 (3): 232–251.

Pérez, Raúl. 2013 "Learning to Make Racism Funny in the 'Color-Blind' Era: Stand-Up Comedy Students, Performance Strategies, and the (re)Production of Racist Jokes in Public." *Discourse & Society* 24(4) 478–503.

Poehler, Amy. 2014. *Yes Please*. New York, NY: Dey Street Books.

Richmond, Ray. 2013. "How Tina Fey's '30 Rock' Lasted Seven Seasons And Changed The Game For Female Comedy Creators." *Deadline*. http://deadline.com/2013/01/30-rock-finale-tina-fey-how-it-changed-tv-417909/

Roiphe, Katie. 2011. "Tina Fey's Tough Girl Feminism." *Slate*. http://www.slate.com/articles/double_x/doublex/2011/03/tina_feys_tough_girl_feminism.html

Sex and the City. 1998–2004. Television Series. Seasons 1–6. USA: HBO.

Shifman, Limor, and Dafna Lemish. 2010. "Between Feminism and Fun(ny)mism: Analyzing Gender in Popular Internet Humor." *Information, Communication and Society* 13(6): 870–891.

Shifman, Limor, and Dafna Lemish. 2011. "'Mars and Venus' in Virtual Space: Post-Feminist Humor and the Internet." *Critical Studies in Media Communication* 28 (3): 253–273.

The Mindy Project. 2012–present. Television Series. Seasons 1–4. USA: FOX/HULU.

Valentini, Valentina. 2015. "Lena Dunham on Why She's an Imperfect Feminist." *The Cut*. http://nymag.com/thecut/2015/04/lena-dunham-on-why-shes-an-imperfect-feminist.html

Vandaele, Jeroen. 2002. "Humor Mechanisms in Film Comedy: Incongruity and Superiority." *Poetics Today* 23 (2): 221–249.

Woodberry, Jazmine. 2013. "6 Simple Reasons Why Amy Poehler Is Today's Feminist Icon." *Mic*. http://mic.com/articles/63901/6-simple-reasons-why-amy-poehler-is-today-s-feminist-icon

Appendix

Interview Guide

1. Introduce yourself and say which of the [four] television shows you watch regularly.
2. Tell me about _____ (discuss each woman/show).
3. How do you watch these shows? (When, with who, via what technology?)
4. If you watch more than one of these shows, which is your favorite? Why?
5. In general, what do you like about these shows?
6. Was there any particular reason that you started watching these shows?
7. How do these shows compare to other sit-coms or dramedies—do these shows stand out from others in their genres?
8. What's funny about these shows?
9. How would you describe the main characters in these shows?
10. When you watch these shows, is there a character that you most identify with? Which character would you say is your favorite? Why?
11. For shows that have finished what did you think/feel about the series finales?
12. How do you think that the fact that the showrunners are women affects the portrayal of gender in these shows?
13. Do you follow any of the showrunners in other media formats? If so, where/through what? And why?
14. Sometimes these shows are described as "feminist." Do you think these are feminist shows? Why/why not?
15. Is there anything I didn't ask you that you'd like to share with me?

Orange Is the New Black: the popularization of lesbian sexuality and heterosexual modes of viewing

Katerina Symes

ABSTRACT

The Netflix original series *Orange Is the New Black* (*OITNB*) is ushering in an identifiable genre of crossover television programming through its popularization of queer content. One of the noteworthy elements about this programme is the extent to which it invites female viewers who self-identify as heterosexual to interact with forms of queer media that they would not necessarily seek out otherwise. This paper explores the invitational structure of *OITNB*, alongside the new structures of distribution for television content, to address how straight-identified women are invited to watch and engage with lesbian sexuality. It examines and critiques how the character Piper Chapman is constituted as a heterosexual proxy for straight-identified women's entry into the world of queer sexuality within the fictional Litchfield Penitentiary.

Introduction

In the 2013 pilot episode of *Orange Is the New Black* (*OITNB*), the audience is introduced to Piper Chapman (Taylor Schilling), a white, upper-middle class, thirty-something woman living in New York City. Sitting in her parents' living room alongside her fiancée Larry (Jason Biggs), Piper explains her recent drug trafficking conviction to her family, revealing that ten years ago she transported a suitcase of drug money to her former girlfriend and international drug smuggler Alex Vause (Laura Prepon). Bewildered, her mother asks in disbelief "You were a lesbian?" to which Piper responds "At the time." Unconvinced by Piper's confession, her brother questions "You still a lesbian?" Resigned, and perhaps slightly ambivalent, Piper replies "No, I am not still a lesbian." In an attempt to relieve the tension, Larry interjects with a sarcastic and seemingly inappropriate remark: "You sure?" Piper's assertion that she is "not still a lesbian" alongside her engagement to Larry may serve to construct her previous relationship with Alex as either experimental or simply a phase. However, the ambiguity in her statement (it is an indication of what she *is not*—a negation of what others assume her sexual identity to be—rather than a confirmation of what she *is*) cannot but suggest that Piper's presumed heterosexuality is perhaps a much more complicated sexually identified position that it may initially seem.

There has been a recent proliferation of television programmes engaging with lesbian representational content, including the Netflix original series *OITNB*. Debuting in July 2013, *OITNB* is based on Piper Kerman's 2010 memoir *Orange Is the New Black: My Year in a Women's Prison* and was created by track-record television writer and producer Jenji Kohan. One of the show's noteworthy elements is its crossover appeal. Through its engagement with queer content, *OITNB* invites female viewers who self-identify as heterosexual to interact with forms of queer media that they would not necessarily seek out otherwise (such as a queer film festival). Indeed, lesbian characters have arguably always been on television (Lynne Joyrich 2001; Anna McCarthy 2001; Amy Villarejo 2014); however, unlike other programmes that include lesbian characters[1] *OITNB* depicts a multiplicity of body types that includes a range of characters with overlapping gender (e.g., cis, trans, masculine, femme, butch), sexual (e.g., lesbian, queer, heterosexual, heteroflexible), class (e.g., working, upper-middle), and racial and ethnic identities (e.g., African American, Caucasian, Dominican, Puerto Rican). *OITNB* ushers in an identifiable genre of crossover television programming through its engagement with queer content. The show contests the heteronormativity of network television by inviting female, straight-identified audiences to explicitly engage with lesbian characters that represent a wide range of gender performances, and class, racial, and ethnic positions. The character of Piper Chapman thus serves as an entry point into the world of queer sexuality in *OITNB* by encouraging straight-identified women to both watch and identify with her character. This paper complicates this normative argument by suggesting that Piper's subsequent queering in future episodes ultimately leads straight-identified women into a more complicated sexually identified position.

Part of *OITNB*'s appeal to diversity stems from the fact that the series is one of Netflix's original programmes. Unlike shows that air on commercial broadcasting networks, the writers and producers of programmes distributed by the on-demand Internet streaming service are not necessarily required to make the same types of representational concessions to advertisers (Jonathan Gray 2008). Instead, *OITNB* can be viewed as part of a recent proliferation of what Jason Mittell (2015) refers to as complex television—elaborate forms of narrative programming facilitated by changes in new technologies and modes of distribution that challenge the episodic and serial conventions of American television. *OITNB*'s narrative complexity retains a heightened degree of self-consciousness that demands more formally aware modes of viewing. For instance, the show uses nonlinear modes of serial narration such as individual character flashbacks to weave long-term story arcs within clearly defined episodic parameters. Part of the viewers' task is to piece together the elaborate backstories of the show's characters. The very first scene in *OITNB* opens with a montage of various bathing and shower scenes of Piper throughout the years—something that is only inferred after the sequence ends in the present day timeline wherein Piper is in prison and the voice-over narrator is revealed to be her. At the outset, then, *OITNB* demands viewers' intensified engagement at the level of form, as it is both a structural condition of the show and one of its pleasures.

This practice of formally aware viewing is only further facilitated by the bingeing and re-watching opportunities afforded by Netflix's decision to release an entire season of programming all at once into its digital library. As Mittell (2015) suggests,

> today's complex narratives are designed for a discerning viewer not only to pay close attention to once but to rewatch in order to notice the depth of references, to marvel at the displays of craft and continuities, and to appreciate details that require the liberal use of pause and rewind. (2015, 38)

Successive and multiple viewings are thus conditions of possibility for engaging with *OITNB*'s narrative complexity.

As a non-normative show (both in form and content), *OITNB* appeals to a range of viewers:[2] those who value edgy, queer, urbane material; viewers of prison dramas; readers of Kerman's memoir; fans of Kohan's previous series *Weeds*; Netflix subscribers who enjoy the service's original programming, and so on. *OITNB* thus represents a shift in both industry and viewers' expectations of what constitutes a hit television show.[3] In today's television landscape "a consistent cult following of a small but dedicated audience can suffice to make a series economically viable" (Mittell 2015, 34).

While *OITNB*'s appeal to a specific range of viewers may represent a shift in the television landscape, it simultaneously represents a tension inherent to the popularization of queer content. In terms of the show's content, its representational diversity may reflect an interest by the show's writers and producers to most accurately representing the multiplicity of queer life.[4] However, the effects of this diversity continue to be assessed on the basis of marketing and other bottom-line demands: *OITNB*'s commercial viability is to some extent contingent upon its ability to attract a range of viewers, not simply those for whom edgy, queer, urbane material is of interest. Additionally, queer critical accounts have widely critiqued *OITNB* as a means by which the television industry has attempted to cash in on the burgeoning queer market (Danae Clark 1993; Amy Gluckman and Betsy Reed 1997; Rosemary Hennessy 1995, 2000). Popular critiques argue that the *OITNB* panders to a male gaze by indulging in the lesbian prison fantasy, while others suggest that the show only depicts particular types of women—thin, young, and predominantly white—either nude or engaging in sexually explicit activities (Noah Gittell 2014). Thus, *OITNB* may increase the visibility of previously marginalized identities; however, its crossover appeal may reproduce a heterosexist understanding of sexuality wherein queer characters continue to be typified in specific ways.

Under these terms, it becomes noteworthy to consider *OITNB*'s invitational structure. Audiences no longer have to search for the hidden signs and codes of lesbian sexuality or engage in resistant readings of dominant or popular culture, as *OITNB* includes a range of characters with complex gender and sexual identities. The question then becomes: how are female, straight-identified audiences invited to both watch and engage with queer content?

An invitation to watch: Piper Chapman as heterosexual proxy

> In a lot of ways Piper was my Trojan Horse. You're not going to go into a network and sell a show on really fascinating tales of black women, and Latina women, and old women and criminals. But if you take this white girl, this sort of fish out of water, and you follow her in, you can then expand your world and tell all of those other stories … The girl next door, the cool blonde, is a very easy access point, and it's relatable for a lot of audiences and a lot of networks looking for a certain demographic. (Jenji Kohan, *NPR's Fresh Air*)[5]

As a programme with queer crossover content, *OITNB* acknowledges its female, straight-identified audience by establishing the character of Piper Chapman as a heterosexual proxy; Piper serves as an entry point into the world of queer sexuality by inviting straight-identified women to both watch and identify with her character. The following section outlines how Piper as heterosexual proxy caters to straight-identified women through the creation of normative viewing positions—namely, voyeurism and sexual or identity tourism. I complicate this normative argument by suggesting that Piper's subsequent queering in future episodes leads straight-identified women into a more complicated sexually identified position—one that has the potential to challenge normative heterosexuality.

In the first few episodes of *OITNB*, Piper is positioned as heterosexual. Although the first scene may reveal in a flashback that Piper was previously in a relationship with another woman, Alex, her present-day engagement to her fiancé Larry—the primary timeline wherein *OITNB* takes place—serves to re-affirm that Piper is "not still a lesbian." This positioning of Piper as "not still a lesbian" constructs her as presumably heterosexual.[6] Her character serves as an invitation for viewers to both watch and identify with her whiteness, class privilege, and heterosexuality, as she narrowly approximates white, straight-identified women viewers' own gender and sexual identities.

OITNB's narrative and formal elements further reinforce Piper as a point of identification for straight-identified women. Piper's narrative is the initial entry point into the world of Litchfield Penitentiary, and audiences witness their first same-sex encounter through her character in the pilot episode "I Wasn't Ready." In this scene, Piper is still new to prison life; she is depicted moving slowly and deliberately through the bathroom, taking in her surroundings. As she makes her way past the toilets, she hears a woman yelling in Spanish behind a closed stall, the other inmates unphased by the commotion. Curious, Piper pauses and bends over to catch a glimpse of the woman before we hear the sound of a toilet flushing. The door swings open and Piper stares with a child-like fascination as Blanca Flores (Laura Gómez) exits. It is not long before Blanca notices Piper staring, meeting her gaze with a "Boo!" Startled, Piper scurries off. As she makes her way to the exit, this time looking down at her feet, something catches her attention from the corner of her eye. Once again, Piper pauses as she slowly looks to her left. The shot cuts to a medium-long shot (from Piper's point-of-view) of two inmates—Nicky Nichols (Natasha Lyonne) and Lorna Morello (Yael Stone)—having sex in the shower as the non-diegetic sound of a bass guitar (reminiscent of a late 1970s porno film) begins to swell. The shot cuts back to Piper as she looks away, trying not to stare. But Piper's eyes cannot help but wander, and we see her once again look slowly over to her left. This time, the shot cuts to a close-up of Morello's face (again, from Piper's point-of-view), who appears to be on the edge of orgasm. The camera pans down Morello's body and stops on Nicky—her faced buried between Morello's legs. Nicky looks up coyly at Piper, meeting her gaze. Caught staring once again, Piper looks away and exits the bathroom.

Through Piper, this scene provides audiences a glimpse into the perhaps unfamiliar yet titillating world of lesbian sexual expression (Kristen A. Crites 2006; Gray 2008). Because Piper is positioned as "not still a lesbian" at this point in the narrative, she offers a point of identification for straight-identified women through her approximation of viewers' gender and sexual identities. Additionally, the camera work and editing encourage audiences to adopt Piper's eye-line as their own (Candace Moore 2007). The shot-reverse-shot technique sutures the viewer's gaze to the look of the camera/Piper's point-of-view, wherein the viewer sees what Piper sees. Thus, it is the combination of narrative and formal elements in this scene that invites straight-identified women to engage with lesbian sex safely from Piper's own distant and voyeuristic viewing (i.e., the straight perspective to which they are accustomed).

This positioning of Piper as heterosexual proxy exceeds the masculinist and patriarchal system of desire; it challenges the primacy of the male gaze by making space for women to experience voyeuristic pleasure in lesbian sex. Despite this affordance, Piper's construction as a point of identification is one that is based on somewhat limited and normatively pre-scribed terms wherein sexual orientation is assumed to be the primary vector for identifica-tion. In other words, because straight-identified women do not share the same sexual orientation as the lesbian characters on screen, viewers are only able to identify with heter-osexual characters (i.e., Piper) that narrowly approximate their own gender and sexual iden-tities (Paula Graham 2006). *OITNB* can thus only offer a voyeuristic glimpse into the lives of lesbian women precisely because the normative dimensions of dominant (and dichotomous) gender and sexual constructions remain intact (Crites 2006; Gray 2008).

The tacit assumption of such accounts of viewership is that the position of the audience remains unchanged by the act of watching. Straight-identified women's identifications—either with the characters or with the show itself—do not shift; viewers are interpellated into fixed, unitary, and contingent positions of identification and desire based on their gender and sexual identities, as it is assumed that identification necessitates stable and essential notions of identity (Judith Mayne 1993). Under these terms, viewers' voyeurism never slips into something else; it exists only at the level of fantasy. Such analyses not only foreclose a discussion of how *OITNB* may address straight-identified women differently based on the social, cultural, and subjective positions (i.e., gender, race, class, sexuality, etc.) within which they are situated, but also undermine the very identity politics that support this programme: that seeing positive representations of lesbian characters may have transformative effects on cultural norms.

Indeed, Piper may initially offer a voyeuristic entry point into the world of lesbian sexuality; however, her position is queered in future episodes. (Piper is depicted hooking up with her former girlfriend Alex, who is also serving time at Litchfield for a similar drug trafficking sentence.) While straight-identified viewers may simply extend the voyeurism in previous episodes to Piper's own same-sex encounters, her subsequent queering has the potential to lead viewers into a more complicated sexually identified position.

Piper's queering has the potential to constitute her as a safely ambiguous place from which straight-identified women can experiment with same-sex desire through more homo-voyeuristic or heteroflexible modes of viewing (Sheri L. Manuel 2009; Moore 2007). As men-tioned above, because *OITNB* encourages audiences to initially adopt Piper's eye-line as their own, this queering of Piper's straight perspective subsequently queers straight-identified women's own viewing positions. Rather than maintain a distant and removed voyeurism, straight-identified audiences may engage in fantasy and role-playing opportunities wherein Piper's desire for other women may be adopted (Moore 2007).

Piper's queering may offer straight-identified women the opportunity to share in the same queer sensibility with which queer-identified viewers are already familiar; however, her presence in these same-sex encounters enables audiences to disavow their feelings of same-sex desire (Moore 2007). Piper may be depicted hooking up with Alex in prison, but at no point does she explicitly name her sexual orientation. The only naming of Piper's sex-uality occurs when the other characters attempt to identify and make sense of her sexual orientation based on her contradictory actions and behaviours, which Piper repeatedly refutes. For instance, in the episode entitled "The Chickening," Piper's friend Polly expresses concern that Piper might "turn gay again." Piper challenges the idea, stating "You don't just turn gay. You fall somewhere on a spectrum, like a Kinsey scale" (*Orange Is The New Black* 2013–2016). Piper's queering thus represents an *un*symbolizable moment of same-sex desire for straight audiences; she stands in for an incapacity to render her own sexuality intelligible, as she herself is somewhere between her supposedly heterosexual relationship with Larry and her desire for her former girlfriend Alex. Through Piper, then, straight-identified women are offered a safely ambiguous proxy for experimentation wherein they may adopt Piper's desire for other women as their own through a kind of sexual or identity tourism.

While the fantasy and role-playing opportunities Piper provides through sexual or identity tourism may acknowledge the possibility for straight-identified women to experience desire for lesbian characters, it articulates a specific state set of fantasy. Sexual or identity tourism assumes identification to be a largely conscious process: that viewers possess the capacity to privilege one vector or social identity (i.e., race, gender, class, sexuality) in order to identify with a character that approximates their own identities (Dana Heller 2006). Moreover, Piper's ambiguous sexual orientation provides straight-identified women with the opportunity to disavow their experience of same-sex desire as one that contradicts their avowed hetero-sexual identity external to the viewing process. Like the voyeurism Piper inoculates, sexual or identity tourism thus constructs straight-identified women as necessarily pre-queer; the assumption is that viewers remain unchanged by the act of watching—which is to say that straight-identified women's experience of same-sex desire is one that does not have trans-formative effects on cultural norms.

Although Piper's presence may make this act of disavowal possible, the inclusion of other same-sex encounters in *OITNB* complicates this process. Before Piper herself begins hooking up with Alex in prison, the audience is privy to another sexual encounter between Nicky and Morello. The scene takes place in the prison chapel, and opens with a shot of a stained-glass window before the camera pans down to a medium-long shot of Nicky and Morello having sex. While this scene consists of similar close-up and medium-long shots to those used in the initial shower scene, the look of the camera remains unsutured to either char-acter's perspective. The audience's eye-line is the look of the camera, as the camera's position locates the audience as spectators in the chapel watching Nicky and Morello.

The less heteroflexible viewer may simply extend the voyeurism of the first shower scene to this encounter; she may either refuse or repress (or even simply not experience) any feelings of same-sex desire. However, Piper's absence as the straight-identified audiences' safely ambiguous proxy—which becomes all the more commonplace as the series develops and depicts different same-sex couplings—has important implications: it has the potential to produce a contradiction in the more heteroflexible viewer. With no tenable site of iden-tification, heteroflexible viewers may find it difficult to disavow their potential experience of same-sex desire as touristic. That Morello self-identifies as heterosexual in some ways constructs her as an additional proxy for audiences.[7] However, the primacy given to Piper's narrative, in addition to the fact that the show's formal elements have encouraged audiences to adopt her eye-line as their own at the outset, would suggest that Piper continues to be our primary entry point into the world of lesbian sexuality within Litchfield. If we recall, it is Piper who introduces the audience to Nicky and Morello in the first place. Thus, any potential experience of same-sex desire (if at all) on behalf of the heteroflexible viewer in this scene not only contradicts their avowed heterosexual identities, but also exceeds the heteronor-mative structure of identification and desire.

While Piper's positioning as heterosexual proxy may initially be based on normatively prescribed terms, it perhaps functions as a ruse to invite straight-identified women to engage in different types of viewership—one wherein *OITNB* ultimately leads viewers into a much more sexually complicated position. The following sections examine how straight-identified women may exceed the ways in which *OITNB* addresses them as normatively gendered and sexed subjects. In doing so, I suggest that Piper's subsequent queering retroactively reveals how her initial positioning as heterosexual proxy is both normatively prescribed and perhaps untenable at the outset.

Re-defining reception within television studies

Although *OITNB* may acknowledge straight-identified audiences through voyeurism and identity or sexual tourism, such limited theorizations of the desire straight-identified women experience stem from the emphasis on active (i.e., conscious) modes of viewing within Television and Cultural Studies. While the conscious dimensions of viewing remain important to an analysis of the ways in which straight-identified audiences watch, they unintentionally obscure the unconscious psychic processes that also impact how viewers watch or invest in such shows (Jackie Stacey 1994). The emphasis on viewers' capacities to choose how they engage with cultural texts does not account for the possibility that viewers may also watch in very different ways that are unanticipated both by the modes of address in the show *and* by straight-identified women themselves.

OITNB presumes at the very least a viewer who engages with queer content. However, this engagement may be largely unconscious for viewers who identify as straight, as the experience of same-sex desire is one that is contradictory, and may be either repressed or displaced during conscious modes of viewing. Thus, it becomes difficult to assume that audiences possess the capacity to privilege certain vectors of social identity (i.e., gender and sexuality) in their identifications with either the show or a set of characters (i.e., Piper), as these investments many not necessarily be consciously apprehended (Heller 2006).

In order to account for the complex ways straight-identified audiences are invited to watch programmes with queer crossover content, it becomes necessary to re-theorize psychoanalytic spectator theory in light of both the popularization of queer sexuality and the new structures of distribution for television content. The final sections of this paper reimagine a spectatorial subject position for female, straight-identified viewers of *OITNB*. As I will suggest, theorizing the specificity of spectatorial positioning is crucial for rethinking the terms of televisual watching; it not only acknowledges how *OITNB* may address spectators, but also accounts for the ways in which the specificity of one's spectatorial positioning may exceed this very address.

Theorizing the specificity of spectatorial positioning

OITNB may address straight-identified audiences through the creation of specific viewing positions—namely, voyeurism and identity or sexual tourism; however, this address does not solely determine the spectator's possibilities for identification and desire. For straight-identified audiences, watching *OITNB* always already involves a process of identification. As Teresa De Lauretis (1984) suggests, each spectator comes to the viewing process with a specific personal and social semiotic history—"a series of previous identifications by which she or he has been somehow en-gendered." The images on screen are not simply "neutral object[s] of pure perception," but rather "significant images," as each spectator brings her own social, cultural, and subjective experiences to the act of watching (145). This specificity affords each spectator a particular line of vision from which to look, interpret, and identify. The codes and social formations of the televisual apparatus may define positions of meaning; however, the spectator is able to rework these positions into a personal and subjective construction. Put differently, the televisual address speaks to each individual spectator differently based on the social, cultural, and subjective (conscious and unconscious) positions within which she is situated, which presents spectators with different affordances and constraints in terms of identification and desire. The viewing process is thus neither fixed nor entirely conscious, but rather continuous and provisional; the spectator's personal and subjective experiences both inform and are informed by her engagement with the image on screen, as it is the complex nexus of effects between social, historical, and subjective (conscious and unconscious) experiences that offer the spectator specific—yet, shifting—viewing positions and self-images.

Extending De Lauretis' reflections to *OITNB*, I maintain that voyeurism and identity or sexual tourism are not necessarily the only viewing positions by which straight-identified audiences both watch the show and engage with queer sexuality. *OITNB* may address audiences as normatively gendered and sexed subjects; however, this address may be both experienced and reworked differently based on the specificity of each individual's subjective position. The specificity of spectatorial positioning[8] presents the conditions of possibility for straight-identified spectators to engage in processes of identification and desire that exceed the current heteronormative structure; spectatorial identifications are not necessarily dependent on the search for one's self on screen—a position that is prescribed by both normative (i.e., stable and essential) notions of gender and sexuality.

Acquiring a queer sensibility without a heterosexual proxy

The potentially transformative effects of straight-identified spectators' engagement with queer sexuality in *OITNB* could not be more evident than in the same-sex encounters where Piper is not present. As mentioned above, Piper's absence may at first be disconcerting for the straight-identified spectator; however, I maintain that her presence is no longer needed. While the female, straight-identified spectator may have gained entry into the world of lesbian sexuality through the heterosexual proxy of Piper, her successful enculturation into this world (through both the show's form and content) now presents her with the possibility to access this newfound queer sensibility on her own, independent of a heterosexual proxy.

Rather than experience same-sex desire through a heterosexual proxy alone, straight-identified spectators now possess the capacity to experience this desire through multiple points of identification. To return to Nicky and Morello's second sex scene in the chapel, we can see that the camera work and editing contradict the narrative assumption that Morello is simply experimenting. While Morello puts an end to her sexual relationship with Nicky immediately after she orgasms, it is important to note that the look of the camera remains unsutured to either character's perspective in this scene; the look of the camera is the spectator's own gaze, positioning her inside the church with them. The camera work and editing explicitly invite the straight-identified spectator to watch and take part in this scene, as much as the show's narrative attempts to excuse Morello's behaviour as a momentary lapse in her supposedly heterosexual identity.

These techniques are used in the numerous other same-sex encounters depicted throughout the series, from Nicky's sexual liaisons with other Litchfield inmates (whose identities, let alone sexual orientations, remain unclear) to Piper's own kiss with new inmate Stella

Carlin (Ruby Rose) in season three[9]—the same season where she and Alex agree to be in a relationship. In these instances, then, it is the complex nexus of effects between *OITNB*'s narrative and formal elements that constitutes the terms and positionalities of identification and desire for spectators (De Lauretis 1984). The straight-identified spectator is able to experience same-sex desire through a point of identification that extends beyond the search for one's approximate self on screen precisely because she exceeds the heteronormative structure of identification and desire—a position that may be initially offered (although not exclusively) by taking on Piper as a heterosexual proxy.

The acquisition of this queer sensibility is only further encouraged by the fact that the show's narrative complexity necessitates more formally aware modes of viewing. As mentioned above, part of one's task when viewing a nonlinear show like *OITNB* is to piece together the characters' elaborate backstories within the present day narrative by bingeing and re-watching the series. Perhaps one of the many pleasures of *OITNB* is the discovery that Piper's sexuality—and by extension her position as heterosexual proxy—is not as determined as it may initially seem. For instance, if we re-watch Nicky and Morello's first shower scene with this newfound queer sensibility, alongside the knowledge that Piper's position is subsequently queered in future episodes, we can see that Piper's voyeuristic position is under erasure at the outset. Instead of a distant and removed voyeurism, Piper's gaze may now be reflective of an act of curious contemplation. The cut to her point-of-view would now suggest that her gaze is perhaps deliberate and intentional; she looks because she perhaps desires to join Nicky and Morello in the shower.

This retroactive reading thus reveals Piper's sexuality to be anything but stable, as it now contradicts the initial narrative assumption that Piper is straight. The combination of bingeing and re-watching not only makes possible more heteroflexible modes of viewership, but also reveals how the experience of same-sex desire re-orients the straight-identified spectator's relationship to her past and present viewing experiences (Patricia White 1999). Rather than maintain a distant and voyeuristic viewing position, straight-identified viewers may now be more willing to join *in* the shower and adopt Piper's desires as their own. This retroactively acquired queer sensibility now invites spectators to enter the shower along with Piper, even if only at the level of fantasy.

Piper as heterosexual proxy: untenable from the outset?

Piper's position as a heterosexual proxy thus functions to retroactively reveal how such a position is in fact untenable. If the straight-identified spectator is able to both acquire and extend this queer sensibility to both past and subsequent episodes of *OITNB* (and perhaps even to other popular crossover programmes), it may be possible for the spectator to position herself outside of the initial voyeuristic position at the outset: that is, the straight-identified spectator may enter this world of lesbian sexuality through a viewing position that differs from the initial voyeuristic entry point of Piper.

OITNB may make space for both voyeuristic and heteroflexible modes of viewing—one can either stay back and watch from a distance, or share in the queer sensibility by joining Nicki and Morello in the shower. However, Piper's sexual ambiguity ultimately renders the initial heterosexual voyeurism promised in this shower scene as an untenable site of identification for the female, straight-identified spectator. We come to understand that Piper's desire no longer fits within the current heteronormative structure; her voyeurism becomes too implicated, her pleasure too visible—and yet, at the outset, the self-identified heterosexual woman continues to watch.

The show itself acknowledges this shift in Piper's position as heterosexual proxy by de-privileging her narrative. While Piper's narrative may have served as entry point into the world of Litchfield, in later episodes it is no longer set up to be the primary narrative through which the other characters' stories unfold. By season three, her story arc becomes one of many intersecting vignettes being told by the show itself. At the formal level, then, this structural shift not only challenges Piper's initial positioning as heterosexual proxy, but also questions whether or not such a position is even needed for straight-identified spectators at the outset since a queer sensibility can subsequently be both acquired and maintained without her.

Piper may inoculate a specific mode of viewership—namely, to provide a narrative entry point for the heterosexual spectator into the world of lesbian sexuality within Litchfield; however, her own shifting identifications provide a critical space wherein the straight-identified spectator may experience the complex and potentially transformative effects of engaging with queer content. The straight-identified spectator is in fact implicated in multiple ways; Piper as heterosexual proxy is but one means by which straight-identified spectators may engage with lesbian sexuality, as *OITNB*'s invitational structure—both in form and content—also assists in the enculturation of a queer sensibility. Thus, stepping outside normative heterosexuality is perhaps a condition of possibility for straight-identified spectators when viewing programmes with queer crossover content. After all, it takes a certain type of heterosexual spectator to watch a show like *OITNB* at the outset—one who understands (either consciously or unconsciously) that she is tuning in to watch a show about lesbian women and lesbian desire.

Conclusion

The straight-identified spectator's ability to acquire a queer sensibility necessitates a more complex approach to how we might image the interrelationship between identification, desire, and queer content. A show like *OITNB* may address straight-identified women as normatively gendered and sexed subjects; however, this address does not solely determine spectators' possibilities for identification and desire. Thus, the acquisition of this queer sensibility is a position that is not necessarily available to all spectators at the outset of viewing; the modes of address speak to the spectators differently, reorienting their memory of and relationship to their past and present viewing experiences (White 1999). Engaging with queer sexuality thus has potentially transformative effects, as the specificity of one's spectatorial position is always changing.

Unlike voyeurism or identity or sexual tourism—positions that necessitate stable notions of identity—this retroactive acquisition of a queer sensibility is *eccentric*; it is a space wherein the straight-identified spectator is able to exceed how she is addressed as a normatively gendered and sexed subject, presenting her with different positionalities for identification and desire that exceed the search for one's self on screen (Teresa De Lauretis 2007). Such a viewing position rests on the very decentring of normative heterosexuality, as the straight-identified spectator must step outside the confines of the current heteronormative structure of identification and desire. In other words, it is the specificity of the appeal to

FEMINIST RECEPTION STUDIES IN A POST-AUDIENCE AGE

flexibility in *OITNB* that not only upsets normative categories of gender and sexuality, but also constitutes the transformative effect of the show for spectators who experience same-sex desire, perhaps for the very first time.

Notes

1. Many shows airing on commercial broadcasting networks (*Ellen*, *Friends*, *Glee*, etc.) have a tendency to relegate lesbian characters to either a marginal or token role within a series. While *The L Word* was one of the first programmes to include multiple lesbian characters as part of the series' primary narrative, it was extensively critiqued for its lack of diversity; many of the lesbian characters were white, upper-middle class, able-bodied, and hegemonically feminine.

2. Ted Sarandos (2014)—Netflix's chief content officer—has noted in an interview that one would be hard-pressed to find an unconventional show (both in form and content) like *OITNB* on either network or cable television, which would perhaps suggest that the show appeals to a specific demographic of viewers for whom such content and formal challenges are of interest. Sarandos has also stated that *OITNB* appeals to a different demographic of viewers than some of the other original programmes offered by the on-demand Internet streaming service (i.e., *House of Cards*). However, there is a degree of overlap in viewership. Despite this crossover audience, *OITNB*'s viewership has a tendency to be skewed toward more young and female audiences.

3. According to Nielsen, 6.7 million people watched the *OITNB*'s season-four premiere from June 17 (its premiere) to June 19, 2016. These numbers place *OITNB* in the same league as some of cable's most watched television shows, such as HBO's *Game of Thrones*, which had 10.4 million total viewers for its June 19 episode (see Daniel Holloway 2016).

4. In an interview with *National Public Radio* (*NPR*), Kohan has discussed her interest in having *OITNB* tell different stories from a range of women with overlapping gender, sexual, class, and racial and ethnic positions (see Jenji Kohan 2013).

5. *National Public Radio's* (*NPR*) *Fresh Air* interview with Jenji Kohna entitled "'Orange' Creator Jenji Kohan: 'Piper Was My Trojan Horse.'" Air date: August 13, 2013.

6. The ambiguity in Piper's statement gestures toward her subsequent queering in future episodes—something audiences are not necessarily privy to during their first viewing of the series. At this point in the narrative, it is thus possible to assume that Piper is heterosexual, as she affirms that she is "not still a lesbian."

7. Morello in fact ends her sexual relationship with Nicky immediately after she orgasms in this scene. Her reasoning for ending the sexual relationship is twofold: she wants to remain faithful to her fiancée Christopher (who is outside of prison), and thus would like to "tighten up" for her soon-to-be-husband. What is particularly interesting about Morello's reasoning for ending her relationship with Nicky is that it is *not* contingent upon the fact that it is a same-sex sexual relation.

8. Accounting for difference is integral to theorizing the specificity of spectatorial positioning in relation to how straight-identified spectators are invited to watch programmes with queer "crossover" content like *OITNB*. Thus, I will refer to viewers as spectators rather than audiences herein, as the term "audience" not only massifies spectators into an undifferentiated viewing population, but also cannot account for difference both within and between spectators.

9. Other same-sex sexual relations in the series include Alex and Nicky in season one, Poussey Washington (Samira Wiley) and her German girlfriend Franziska (Nina Rausch) in season two, Nicky and Brook Soso (Kimiko Glenn) in season two, the self proclaimed "butch" Big Boo (Lea DeLaria) and an unnamed woman—presumably Big Boo's former girlfriend—in season three, and Poussey Washington (Samira Wiley) and Brook Soso (Kimiko Glenn) in season four.

Disclosure statement

No potential conflict of interest was reported by the author.

Funding

This work was supported by the Social Sciences and Humanities Research Council of Canada.

References

Clark, Danae. 1993. "Commodity Lesbianism." In *The Lesbian and Gay Studies Reader*, edited by Henry Abelove, Michèle Aina Barale, and David M. Haperin, 186-201. London: Routledge.

Crites, Kristen A. 2006. "The L Word." *Journal of GLBT Family Studies* 2 (1): 123–125. Accessed January 20, 2016. doi: 10.1300/J461v02n01_06.

de Lauretis, Teresa. 1984. *Alice doesn't: Feminism, Semiotics, Cinema*. Bloomington: Indiana University Press.

De Lauretis, Teresa. 2007. *Figures of Resistance: Essays in Feminist Theory*, edited by Patricia White. Urbana and Chicago: University of Illinois Press.

Game of Thrones. 2011–2016. Television Series. Season 1–6. USA: HBO.

Gittell, Noah. 2014. "The One Thing that Keeps *Orange is the New Black* from being the Most Feminist Show on Television." *Mic*, July 10, 2014. Accessed January 20, 2016. http://mic.com/articles/93117/the-one-thing-keeping-orange-is-the-new-black-from-being-the-most-feminist-show-on-television?utm_source=policymicFB&utm_medium=main&utm_campaign=social#.feRIM2oEu

Gluckman, Amy, and Betsy Reed. 1997. "The Gay Marketing Moment." In *A Queer World: The Center for Lesbian and Gay Studies Reader*, edited by Martin Duberman, 519–525. New York and London: New York University Press.

Graham, Paula. 2006. "*The L Word* Under-Whelms the UK?" In *Reading The L Word: Outing Contemporary Television*, edited by Kim Akass and Janet McCabe, 15–26. London and New York: I.B. Tauris.

Gray, Jonathan. 2008. *Television Entertainment*. New York and London: Routledge.

Heller, Dana. 2006. "How does a Lesbian Look?: Stendhal's Syndrome and *The L Word*." In *Reading The L Word: Outing Contemporary Television*, edited by Kim Akass and Janet McCabe, 55–68. London and New York: I.B. Tauris.

Hennessy, Rosemary. 2000. *Profit and Pleasure: Sexual Identities in Late Capitalism*. New York and London: Routledge.

Hennessy, Rosemary. 1995. "Queer Visibility in Commodity Culture." In *Social Postmodernism: Beyond Identity Politics*, edited by Linda Nicholson and Steven Seidman, 144–187. Cambridge: Cambridge University Press.

Holloway, Daniel. 2016. "TV Ratings: 'Orange is the New Black' Premiere Numbers Revealed." *Variety*, June 29, 2016. Accessed August 31, 2016. http://variety.com/2016/tv/ratings/tv-ratings-orange-is-the-new-black-premiere-nielsen-1201805991/

House of Cards. 2013–2016. Television Series. Seasons 1–4. USA: Netflix.

Joyrich, Lynne. 2001. "Epistemology of the Console." *Critical Inquiry* 27 (3): 439–467. Accessed January 20, 2016. http://0www.jstor.org.mercury.concordia.ca/stable/134421610.1086/449016

Kerman, Piper. 2010. *Orange Is the New Black: My Year in a Women's Prison*. New York, NY: Spiegel & Grau.

Kohan, Jenji. 2013. "'Orange' Creator Jenji Kohan: 'Piper was My Trojan Horse.'" *NPR's Fresh Air*, August 13, 2013. Accessed August 31, 2016. http://www.npr.org/2013/08/13/211639989/orange-creator-jenji-kohan-piper-was-my-trojan-horse

McCarthy, Anna. 2001. "*ELLEN*: Making Queer Television History." *GLQ* 7 (4): 593-620. Accessed January 20, 2016. doi: 10.1215/10642684-7-4-593.

Manuel, Sheri L. 2009. "Becoming the Homovoyeur: Consuming Homosexual Representations in *Queer as Folk*." *Social Semiotics* 19 (3): 275–291. Accessed January 20, 2016. doi: 10.1080/10350330903072656.

Mayne, Judith. 1993. *Cinema and Spectatorship*. London: Routledge.

Mittell, Jason. 2015. *Complex TV: The Poetics of Contemporary Television Storytelling*. New York and London: New York University Press.

Moore, Candace. 2007. "Having it all Ways: The Tourist, the Traveler, and the Local in The L Word." *Cinema Journal* 46 (4): 3–22. Accessed January 20, 2016. http://0-www.jstor.org.mercury.concordia.ca/stable/30137717.

Orange Is the New Black. 2013-2016. Television Series. Seasons 1-4. USA: Netflix.

Sarandos, Ted. 2014. "The Backstory of Netflix's Biggest Show." *CNN Money*, June 6, 2014. Accessed August 31, 2016. http://money.cnn.com/video/media/2014/06/06/netflix-orange-is-the-new-black-ted-sarandos.cnnmoney?iid=EL

Stacey, Jackie. 1994. *Star Gazing: Hollywood Cinema and Female Spectatorship*. London and New York: Routledge.

Villarejo, Amy. 2014. *Ethereal Queer: Television, Historicity, Desire*. Durham and London: Duke University Press.

White, Patricia. 1999. *unInvited: Classical Hollywood Cinema and Lesbian Representability*. Bloomington and Indianapolis: Indiana University Press.

A queerly normalized Western lesbian imaginary: online Chinese fans' gossip about the Danish fashion model Freja Beha Erichsen

Jing Jamie Zhao

ABSTRACT
Online gossip is an important site of negotiation and contestation for today's global popular culture in the post-audience age. This article presents a discourse analysis of Chinese fans' queer gossip about the Danish female model, Freja Beha Erichsen, in one of the most sizable and influential cyber Chinese fandoms, The Garden of Eden Communication Site for Foreign Series (GE). Erichsen has been famous worldwide for her queer persona and homosocial/ homoerotic relationships. The gossip discussed in the research was mainly produced in GE between September 2007 and December 2012. My examination highlights the ambivalent strategy—namely, queer normalization—employed by GE fans. I show that the fans queerly contested yet also renormalized the commercialized images of Erichsen. Furthermore, I illustrate how GE fans both debated and contradictorily reimagined Erichsen's personal lesbian relationships based on Chinese-specific social-familial and marital ideals pertaining to women's genders and sexualities. Ultimately, I argue that this tendency of GE fans to craft "desirable," "normalized" queer fantasies about Erichsen can be seen as an interesting set of queer strategies that allow the fans to creatively reconfigure these local Chinese normative cultural conventions and traditions as viable models for queer women's survival and expression.

Introduction

Gossip has constantly been trivialized by mainstream patriarchal cultures. Nevertheless, in the post-audience age it constitutes a significant, albeit highly contested, terrain of popular culture. Feminist media studies often see gossip as an active socio-cultural process whereby "situating, interpreting, and transforming [information] … against the background of one's own social position and interests" (Erin Meyers 2010, 5) allows one to reflect on one's own socio-cultural situations and lived experiences (John Champagne and Elayne Tobin 1997, 54). While celebrities are symbols "for the configuration, positioning, and proliferation" of dominant socio-cultural norms and ideologies (David Marshall 1997, 72), fan gossip serves as a creative, performative way of producing new cultures, information, and imaginations;

indeed, it casts light on how prevalent normative ideologies are negotiated in public cultures and spaces (Joshua Gamson 1994; Joke Hermes 1999; Chris Rojek 2001). As Helen Leung elaborated in her study of queer gossip surrounding Hong Kong celebrities, "gossip can function through the mass media as a site for self-*making*, both for the celebrity whom the media is bent on 'outing' and the queer spectators 'in the know'" (2008, 91). Leung's view delimits the self-contradictory aspects of non-Western fans' queer subjective practices that not only negotiate and sometimes even tactically conform to local (hetero)normative popular cultures but also discursively challenge the universalist Western liberal model of queer identities and activism.

Notably, recent Asian queer studies have criticized the "global gay" theory that equates queer globalization in Asia with an Asian emulation of a Western/global queer model (Leung 2008; Fran Martin 2011). This article follows this research direction to examine "how elsewheres ... are thought about and imaginatively constituted locally, often in the service of elaborating local queer selves and scenes" (Martin 2011, 118). My analysis explores the multilayered entanglements of queer desires with normative ways of living and thinking in Chinese fans' imagination of Western queer celebrity figures. I present a case study of Chinese fan gossip about the Danish female model, Freja Beha Erichsen, in one of the most sizable and influential cyber Chinese fandoms, The Garden of Eden Communication Site for Foreign Series (GE).[1] My exploration focuses on the problematic, yet critical, gossip moments that epitomize the fans' simultaneous queer contestation and reification of hetero-patriarchal norms in Chinese society, such as those governing local practices of family and marriage.

Built in early 2003 by a group of Chinese fans of Western television shows, GE has become famous for its large number of queer-themed discussion boards and threads devoted to Western celebrities.[2] The site requires email registration to post on its discussions boards but, for viewing, offers open access. Its lesbian discussion board was originally built in early 2005 and remains highly popular in Chinese cyberspace today.[3] The information circulated on this board, including queer-related rumors, news, images, and videos of Western female celebrities, were mostly gathered and/or translated by GE fans from both Chinese- and English-language entertainment media and websites, online celebrity gossip magazines or blogs, and other fan sites. As of January 2016, the board had more than 6,880 threads and 924,000 entries. Most entries are fans' queer gossip. GE's own online surveys indicate that the majority of active fans on this board are young, college-educated, Mandarin-speaking, Mainland Chinese women with diverse sexual orientations.[4] The GE gossip about Erichsen was highly active between September 2007 and December 2012 (see Figure 1).[5]

Born in 1987, Erichsen has been well known for her charismatic tomboyish persona since her debut in runway shows in Paris and Milan in the fall of 2005. Her tall, skinny, pale look, low voice, low-key personality, signature tattoos, norm-defying behaviors, and nonconformist attitudes all work together to distinguish her from other traditionally feminine models with curvaceous bodies in the current fashion industry. As a world-famous fashion model, her high-profiled gender nonconformity and homosocial/homoerotic relationships with a large number of lesbian and bisexual women has regularly attracted media attention from early on. Indeed, media celebration and commercialization of her unconventional gender persona often extended beyond Euro-American high-fashion industries. In June 2006, she appeared on the cover of *Vogue China*. As a campaign girl for the popular fashion brand H&M, her images have also frequently been seen in its advertisements on the streets of China since 2011. All of these render Erichsen's stardom one of the most popular topics in GE.

My examination of the GE gossip devoted to Erichsen's lesbianism unpacks the ways online Chinese fans process queer-related information, realities, and possibilities both locally and globally either to articulate imaginative lesbian scenarios or to make sense of, sometimes contest, socio-culturally "normalized" (Elisabeth Engebretsen 2014) ones. In probing the underlying reasons for and implications of this "queerly normalized" GE gossip, I explore the coexistence of queer subjectivities and normative discursive tendencies in the virtual,

Figure 1. A screen capture of one of the GE threads devoted to Erichsen.

transcultural communicative space. I argue that certain Chinese-specific normative discourses—such as those subjecting adult women to the society's hetero-patriarchal prescriptions of their gendered, sexual, and familial-marital roles—in practice also catalyze an interesting set of queer strategies that allow GE fans both to imagine Western female same-sex desires and intimacy in context-specific terms and to creatively reconfigure these norms as viable models for queer survival and expression.

Methodologically, I employ discourse analysis that emphasizes contextual knowledge (Alexandra Georgakopoulou and Dionysis Goutsos 2004) and the immanence of power relations (Michel Foucault 1982) in the process of meaning making and recirculation across diverse kinds of media communication (John Fiske 1996, 6), from which a person's subjectivity emerges. As Fiske (1996) elaborates, discourse is language in social use; language accented with its history of domination, subordination, and resistance; language marked by the social conditions of its use and its users: it is politicized, power-bearing language employed to extend or defend the interests of its discursive community (1996, 3).

Taking my cue from Fiske, I draw materials from three major GE threads to offer a feminist reading of the queer gossip discourse concerning Erichsen's gender, lesbian sexuality, and relationships, thereby analyzing the interests of the GE community and its embedded power relationships.[6] In so doing, this article brings Chinese women's gender and (homo)sexuality research into conversations with (post-)audience studies to probe the complexity and contradictions of queer fantasies and subjectivities in a virtual, transcultural communicative space that has been largely shaped by the offline, mainstream, still-heteronormative social environment.

I begin my discussion with an overview of contemporary Chinese queer women's socio-cultural situations and scholarly discussions of the tendencies of local Chinese queer practices and communities to tactically negotiate with both local normative ideals and global gay cultures. Then, I explore a similar tendency of "queer normalization" reflected in the ways GE fans read and contested the commercialized images of Erichsen's performed gender and sexuality. Furthermore, I investigate how, in gossiping about her personal romance, GE fans both debated and contradictorily reconfigured certain queerly normalized lesbian genders, sexualities, and qualities. I pay particular attention to the fans' subjective negotiations with Chinese-specific media and public cultures and with China's hetero-patriarchal environment at large, which regulates the social roles of queer women. Through this, I will show that the GE gossip epitomizes both the potentials and paradoxes of fan-made Western lesbian imaginaries.

Chinese queer normalization in an age of globalization

Although homosexuality was decriminalized in 1997 and depathologized in 2001 in official legal and medical discourses, in practice China has yet to become homosexual-friendly, especially in regard to queer women (Travis S. K. Kong 2011; Lisa Rofel 2007). Admittedly, lesbians in Mainland China started gaining public visibility in urban cities in the 1990s. By the early 2000s, online lesbian communicative spaces and offline lesbian social gatherings, movements, conferences, and even dating or wedding events in major Chinese cities have become accessible (Liang Shi 2015, 83); it was also around the same time that coming-out in public spaces and media became a possibility for Chinese LGBT people (Lucetta Y. L. Kam 2013, 56). Although few Chinese female celebrities have openly come out, queer women's images and representations, especially those in online media, have become more "universalized" (Fran Martin 2015) and "mainstreamed" (Lucetta Y. L. Kam 2014) in post-2000 Chinese popular culture.

Nevertheless, both explicit and implicit forms of discrimination, persecution, and stereotyping of non-heterosexuality remain prevalent in Chinese public cultures and mainstream media (Kam 2013, 56–57). Even today, textbooks referring to homosexuality as a curable disease are still circulated in many Chinese universities (Shen Lu and Katie Hunt 2015). Shock therapy remains a commonly used "corrective" treatment for homosexual people in some Chinese hospitals (Danny Walker 2015). Moreover, the party-state's persistent patriarchal traditions, heteronormative institutions, and misogynistic policies make independent living and self-expression more difficult for queer women (Engebretsen 2014; Kam 2013). In general, public visibility and awareness of lesbian culture is significantly less in contemporary Chinese society than that of gay culture (Shi-Yan Chao 2010, 84), and by and large, the entwinement of China's asymmetrical gender system with the influence from Buddhist, Confucianist, and Daoist practices has aggravated the already-unpleasant everyday experience for queer women (Shi 2015).

Meanwhile, research has found a Chinese-specific homonormative culture derived from the modernizing and globalizing process in post-socialist China. For instance, in her discussions of the emergence of cosmopolitan Chinese gay identities, Rofel identifies a "quality discourse" (*suzhi* discourse), which, in local terms, functions to normalize ideas of gay desires and create hierarchical divisions, discriminations, and exclusions within Chinese gay communities through practices of pursuing transnational social networks—such as through creating global gay imaginaries and leading cosmopolitan lives (2007, 104–105). Alternatively, without denying the homonormative hierarchies proliferated within Chinese queer cultures, Ching Yau elaborates on a "close-to-normal" mentality which enables a "continual and thriving existence of non-normative sexual subjects" (2010, 4). As Yau explains, non-normative genders and sexualities are not considered to be "normal" or "natural" (*zhengchangde*) in mainstream Chinese culture. Yet, "being queer or non-straight" is not necessarily the opposite of "being normal" in Chinese contexts. Chinese queer subjects' various practices to get "close-to-normal," such as consciously acting "normal," desiring to fit into mainstream cultures, and performing local normative ideals of gender and sexuality, can pave contradictory ways for them to survive discrimination, pathologization, and stigmatization (Yau 2010, 1–14). Through these queerly normalizing activities, they may "gain more bargaining power" (Yau 2010, 4) in mainstream society. Thus, the cultural specificities and social functions of these revised normative practices should not be overlooked.

In her recent study, Engebretsen (2014) has further developed Yau's viewpoint on queer normalization to understand contemporary Chinese queer women's tactical negotiations with both social-familial and homonormative ideals. Her research finds that many contemporary queer women in urban China pursue "respectable *suzhi* ([good] quality) status" (2014, 19). Engebretsen sees queer women's self-conflicting aspirations to sustain social respectability and to fit into local heteronormative institutions and global homonormative cultures as illustrations of their practical survival strategies and living possibilities within Chinese-specific contexts. As she finds, these subjective, "close-to-normal" practices "made long-term lesbian romance and intimacy on the side possible" (2014, 82). During these processes of queer transforming, performing, and becoming normal subjects and qualified citizens in mainstream Chinese society, "normative ideologies defining 'good' conduct and the 'good life' were to some extent desired as well as derided" (2014, 18). Enlightened by these understandings, my research investigates how and why diverse forms of this culture of queer normalization are recapped in and complicating some Chinese fans' Western lesbian imaginaries in cyberspace.

Crafting a Western lesbian imaginary in GE

Erichsen had not explicitly expressed her lesbian identity in public before late 2011. However, she often wore short, boyish hair and androgynous suits and brought intimate female friends to professional gatherings and high-fashion parties. Additionally, never had she hesitated to take explicitly homoerotic pictures with other female friends and models. Since 2006, she has been famously cast in numerous unfixed gender roles and/or featured in homosocial scenes in fashion designer Karl Lagerfeld's Chanel advertisements. For example, in the Pirelli 2011 calendar by Lagerfeld, Erichsen personified male gods in Greek mythology, including Orpheus, Castor, and Apollo. In Lagerfeld's 2010 Chanel short movie *Remember Now*, Erichsen played the role of the male English musician Mick Jagger, who was famous for his androgynous on-stage performance. Later, in the 2011 Chanel short movie by Lagerfeld titled *The Tale of a Fairy*, Erichsen played a genderless fairy (see Figure 2). While her topless, skinny body exhibited a very ambiguous female bodily curve, her genderless appearance intrigued the leading female character who in a later scene had a sexual encounter with her. Interestingly, despite Lagerfeld's well-known gay identity and pro-gay attitude (Thomas Adamson 2013), GE fans often critically challenged this Western "lesbian chic" media image (Aviva Dove-Viebahn 2007) cast through Lagerfeld's gay male gaze, reacting to it with debates over lesbian genders and sexualities.

Figure 2. A screen capture of Erichsen in the Chanel short film *The Tale of a Fairy*.

For example, during GE's gossip about Erichsen's (often non-normative) gender persona in the commercials, some fans cynically joked that Lagerfeld was a "powerful male GL[7] fan" (*geilide baihenan*) who was sexually attracted to lesbians (zonlomo4 2011) and speculated that he often publicly highlighted Erichsen's potential lesbian identity on purpose (hot1 2011c; weiduoliyademimi 2011c). Some also critiqued that Lagerfeld exploited Erichsen as a "toy-boy" (*nanchong*) (hot1 2011b) or a beautiful male model (JoePortard 2011a). One fan sarcastically said that Lagerfeld did so only to present sensational homoerotic moments of gay males or heterosexual couples (hot1 2011a).

What stirred up more controversy in GE was Lagerfeld's Spring 2011 Chanel campaign, in which Erichsen was portrayed in a traditionally feminine appearance in the print advertisement, lying in bed in a seductive pose with a gay male model, Baptiste Giabiconi. Following the post of this image under the thread, many fans showed great frustration toward Lagerfeld's "straightening" of Erichsen. One fan mocked that the use of a male model in the image turned Chanel into "smelly-nel" (*chou naier*) (kal 2011). The satire here implies that the visual bending of Erichsen's lesbian identity into a straight one and the coupling of her heterosexually with males exposed the ugliness of Chanel's profit-driven manipulation of Erichsen. A few fans felt disappointed by the image's heterosexual connotations that they photoshopped the picture by replacing Giabiconi with some female Chanel models, such as Lily Donaldson, Abby Lee, and Catherine McNeil, who have had intimate friendships with Erichsen for a long time (JoePortard 2011b; weiduoliyademimi 2011a). The GE-remade images, dense with lesbian threesome implications, were quickly circulated to other Chinese and English fan sites.[8]

These fan practices not only interrupted heterosexual imaginaries in mainstream Chinese cultures but also playfully re-scripted the gay male designer's commodification of queer women's gender and sexuality on the stage of global fashion industry. The Western lesbian imaginaries thus circulated in the GE gossip neither simply accept/imitate Western queer cultural patterns nor exemplify a universal model of lesbianism as "a disrupter of heterosexuality, a presence standing outside the conventions of patriarchy, a hole in the fabric of gender dualism" (Bonnie Zimmerman 1992, 4). Instead, the tomboy fantasy produced therein plays *within* but also *against* mainstream hetero-patriarchal ideals by celebrating both Erichsen's lasting tomboyism and rich lesbian romances. I elaborate this point in the foregoing analysis of the tomboy fairy tale repeatedly iterated in the GE gossip.

Re-telling a tomboy fairy tale

Tomboyism in Western contexts usually denotes "an extended childhood period of female masculinity" (Judith Halberstam 1998, 5). Dissimilar from this Western definition, there has been a celebration of tomboyism in post-2000 Chinese media and popular cultural representations of young, masculine female celebrities. Rather than serving as a sign of gender/sexual deviance, the tomboyism of these Chinese celebrities is often neutralized by the media and in their fandoms as illustrations of their lack of socio-cultural sophistication and (sexual) experience (Hui Faye Xiao 2012). However, the transcultural tomboy fantasy created in the GE gossip not only draws on but also diverges from this local queer popular cultural trend.

Erichsen's homeland, Denmark, is widely known in China for Hans Christian Andersen's fairy tales. While Erichsen was commonly referred to by GE fans as "a prince from a fairytale kingdom" (*tonghuaguo laide wangzi*) or "a little prince" (*xiaowangzi*), Denmark was often romanticized by the fans as "a God-like nation" (*shenyiyangde guodu*) for its sexually "free" (*ziyou*) and "open" (*kaifang*) environment (samdream 2011; sousou2 2011c; weiduoliyadem-imi 2011e). As early as 2007, Erichsen's backstage, intimate pictures taken with two other high-fashion female models, Lily Donaldson and Irina Lazareanu, were circulated in GE. Following the posts, fans passionately gossiped about which of the models would become the princess for the tomboy prince. Some wrote that "a prince should be coupled and live with her most beautiful princess" (zoenoah 2007a) and that "it would be very romantic for the prince and the princess to live happily together in the fairytale kingdom Denmark" (hot1 2011e). Later, some fans posted a growing number of intimate pictures of Erichsen with other female models and playfully denoted these models as the prince's "harem" (*hougong*) (bundchen 2007a). One fan speculated that it would be difficult to become one of the con-cubines in Erichsen's harem because Donaldson and Lazareanu occupied Erichsen's "East Palace, West Palace"[9] (*donggong xigong*) and the prince must have more secret lovers outside her palace (bundchen 2007b). Some other fans echoed that Erichsen's concubines would "fight with each other for her love" (*zhengchong*) in the harem because she is so attractive (Fiveandtaty 2011a; zoenoah 2007b). Many playfully suggested that since the prince had so many beautiful, traditionally feminine model pursuers, having threesomes would always be a good choice for her (neutrogena 2007; sea000mus 2011). One fan also commented that some of the models could be the prince's potential "friends with benefits" (*paoyou*) (Fiveandtaty 2011b).

The fans' tomboy fantasy re-situates Erichsen in a hybrid milieu that exposes an interesting mix of memories of imperial China's patriarchal, polygamous past—in which lesbianism was often only imaginable as a stimulator for hetero-marital harmony (Tze-lan Sang 2003, 48–50)—and a popular Occidentalist cultural valorization of Denmark (as well as other mod-ernized Western countries) as a fantasy locale for gender and sexual nonconformists in con-temporary China. As Sang (2003) notes, similar fantasies about "concubine harem" and polygamous lesbianism have been dominant tropes in premodern Chinese textual and media representations of female homoeroticism. Additionally, the fact that most GE fans are also avid consumers of Chinese historical dramas on TV and of both local and global popular cultures helps to explain the de-realized, retrospective backdrop of the fan gossip discourse. For example, while gossiping about Erichsen, one fan even playfully admitted that the gossip about Erichsen's lesbian romance looks like a typical "Chinese Imperial TV drama" (*qinggongju*) (dreamland88 2011c).

This polygamous lesbian romance featuring a promiscuous tomboy at first seems to con-firm a problematic binarist way of thinking deeply seated in Chinese public culture's prev-alent association of both premodern China and the modern West, on the one hand, with female homoeroticism and sexual permissiveness, on the other (Bret Hinsch 1990; Jen-peng Liu and Naifei Ding 2005; Fran Martin 2010). Moreover, recasting this binarist idea that is prevalent in local media and cultural narratives in the fans' Western tomboy fantasy, it also draws on a Confucian ideology that emboldens male promiscuity—especially young liter-atis'—as a sign of gallantry (Shi 2015, 60–61). Seen in this light, it is possible that the ways GE fans imaginatively celebrated Erichsen's romantic and sexual relationships might also partially manifest a fan-based cultural tendency to subscribe to the vestiges of patriarchal imagination and thus treat Erichsen, and possibly tomboys in general, as little more than an imitator of males and her lesbianism as a queer replication of normative forms of heterosexuality. However, as gender and queer theorists have extensively shown, "[t]he replication of heterosexual constructs in non-heterosexual frames brings into relief the utterly constructed status of the so-called heterosexual original" (Judith Butler 1990, 31; also see Halberstam 1998). Therefore, this GE fantasy about tomboyism cannot be deemed as an example of derivative, heterosexual-copying lesbian imaginaries. Rather, it is a unique imagination about queer women that contests contemporary Chinese public culture's hetero-patriarchal expectations of women as much as it has been shaped accordingly. For instance, this constant highlighting of tomboy promiscuity and lesbian polygamy not only signals the charm of tomboy images in GE but also triggered debates over appropriate conduct and character of a "good-quality" tomboy who meets public "imaginations of 'healthy' and 'sunny' representations" of Chinese gay people within a post-socialist *suzhi* discourse (Kam 2013, 90). This debate gave away clues to the possible reasons for some GE fans' preference for this fantasy.

For example, one senior fan, sea000mus, once claimed that everybody liked to see a good-looking tomboy having many "surreal" (*chaoxianshi*) sexual and romantic relationships (2012a). Another active fan, SMILE-VIVI, echoed: "whether to become a womanizer is not that simple. It depends on the context. Every [feminine female model] surrounding [Erichsen] is so beautiful and sexually seductive and willing to have sex with her," which makes it hard for Erichsen to constrain herself sexually (2012b). However, one fan questioned their hyper-eroticized tomboy fantasy by saying that "being unfaithful" (*huaxin*) should not be appreciated as a "desirable quality" in males or females (dr_momo 2012a). Sea000mus responded that although sexual promiscuity was not a good thing, it was the only way to reveal Erichsen's charm (2012b). SMILE-VIVI explained this controversial fantasy about Erichsen in a more elaborated way:

> It is already difficult enough for heterosexuals to persist in love, not to mention lesbians. [Erichsen's] eyes and smiles are as innocent as those of a little kid. I hope she will not get hurt. As long as she is happy, she can change her lesbian partners frequently. Because I believe she is the one who will hold onto it (lesbian identity and desire) to the end. I do not care who would be her last lover. (2012c)

This part of fan discussion intriguingly suggested a complicated feeling of sympathy for tomboys that might be interpreted as a discursive critique of Chinese lesbian realities and public cultural imaginations about lesbianism in general. On the one hand, it discloses the fans' disappointment at the heteronormative social environment in which the possibility and long-term stability of lesbian relationships seems less pleasant and affirmative, even for tomboys in a liberating context. On the other hand, some fans' sympathetic interpretations of this promiscuous tomboy image also indirectly speaks to conventional portrayals of tomboys in Chinese public culture. For instance, Martin (2010) identifies two Chinese-speaking popular narrative modes for tomboy representations. One is the "memorial mode," which creates a lesbian gender distinction in which young femmes will eventually pass their lesbian phase and grow into mature heterosexual women; in such narratives about the adult hetero-marital world's present and future, the tomboys typically do not exist—they often have died or vanished from the femme characters' life and appear only in the adult feminine women's mourning (13–14, 132–135). An alternative popular pattern is the "tomboy melodrama," which "presen[ts] tomboy[s] as protagonist[s]," yet often ghettoizes tomboys (14). Discursively responding to both prevalent narrative patterns, the GE fantasy presents a distinct tomboy-centered romance in which Erichsen is the innocent yet sexually irresistible protagonist whose lesbianism is "congenital" and "permanent" (Martin 2010, 11). Whereas narrating young, normatively feminine models as "temporary" or "situational" lesbians (Martin 2010, 11), some fans, such as SMILE-VIVI, imagined Erichsen's lasting tomboyism and lesbianism as a contrast and a playful challenge to the expected heterosexual roles and desires of female subjects. Indeed, the tomboy fantasy explicitly defies the mainstream society's hetero-patriarchal expectations of adult women's gender and sexual roles and critiques the erasure of adult lesbianism and the cruel realities for tomboys' ghettoized, momentary existence in Chinese media cultures. It is exactly the very close proximity of this GE fans' lesbian imaginary to the presumed-to-be-original local Chinese heteronormative frame that debunks "the mechanism of repudiation in sustaining [heterosexual] identities" (Clare Hemmings 1998, 93) and thus helps overturn these hetero-patriarchal gender and sexual ideals.

Some fans' unease about and debates over desirable qualities for tomboys in lesbian sexual relationships also allude to a deep yearning for producing positive images of tomboys. This ambivalent "close-to-normal" desire among the fans that both contests and sometimes heavily relies on certain hetero-marital and misogynistic conventions can also be found in the gossip concerning the topic of stable lesbian relationships.

Imagining a desirable lesbian family

In March 2011, Erichsen's lesbian romance with the American high-fashion model Arizona Muse was gradually revealed in such venues as European photographers' interviews, Taiwanese fans' blogs, and many European fashion magazines. The news spread in GE immediately and caused heated debates. The fans' opinions about the couple were largely polarized, and the debate soon escalated further and eventually resulted in internal divisions after GE fans found out that Muse was a young single mother who gave birth to a boy in her early twenties.

Some GE fans formed "Mama Party" (*mamadang*. MP hereafter) and celebrated the couple's relationship for the reason that Muse brought a son into Erichsen's life (JoePortard 2011c; Y1017 2011). MP fans claimed that, due to the existence of her son, Muse's status as Erichsen's wife was very "stable" (*wengu*) (kt12117 2011b) and "reasonable" (*heli*) (sunshisunshi 2012a). Some GE fans who were opposed to the two's relationship because Muse was a "turned" lesbian with a heterosexual past, constituted "Cat Party" (*maodang*. CP hereafter). CP fans supported Erichsen getting back together with her previous rumored-to-be girlfriend, the Australian lesbian model Catherine McNeil. A bitter exchange on who would eventually win Erichsen's heart soon initiated between these two groups of fans.

Normative aspirations for finding a qualified femme to play the traditionally-defined "mother and wife" roles and form a stable, wholesome lesbian family with Erichsen—often entangled with some fans' discriminatory attitudes toward bisexual and "poor-quality" femmes—underpinned the nature of the fan debate. MP fans constantly argued that Muse was a typical "virtuous wife and loving mother" (*xianqi liangmu*) (dreamland88 2011a) with a "caring-mother quality" (*renmude qizhi*) (mingmingmingyu 2012) and that she looked like a "rational" (*lizhi*) person for Erichsen, who was getting older and more mature herself (bibo-bibo 2011). While McNeil was described by some MP fans to be an emotionally "immature" (*buchengshu*) person with an "unstable" (*buwending*) career (SMILE-VIVI 2012a), some CP fans supported McNeil for her "authentic" (*chun*) lesbian identity.

Interestingly, many GE fans from both groups constantly expressed the wish that Erichsen would get married to either Muse or McNeil (kt12117 2011a; lois323 2011). Some fans also hoped that Erichsen would eventually end up with Muse and form a dreamy (*menghuan*) "family of three" (*yijiasankou*) in which "prince charming can have a wife and a son" (*baimawangzi youqiyouer*) in the future (hot1 2011d; shitchild 2011). Later, after seeing the frequent public appearance of Erichsen and Muse that confirmed the two's lesbian intimacy, one fan also admitted that since F (Erichsen) becomes more mature [and thus] no longer pursues the young, frivolous (*nianshaoqingkuang de*) love with McNeil, she is now in turn devoted to the peaceful, cozy life of a small family (*pingpingdandan de xiaorizi*) with Mama (Muse) (sousou2 2011a). A few other fans also concurred that this lifestyle can guarantee Erichsen a "happy" (*xingfu kuaile*) life (logmei1009log 2011; weiduoliyademimi 2011d).

One CP fan, nevertheless, admitted that she was excited to see the "family photo" (*quanjiafu*) of Erichsen, Muse, and Muse's son (dr_momo 2012b). Yet, she also insinuated that because Muse was a young female who had a child with a man, she could not be "queer that much" (dr_momo 2012c). Similarly, another CP fan was also worried that Muse's heterosexual past made it easier for her to cheat on Erichsen with good-looking males (sousou2 2011b).

In response to this stereotyping of Muse's potential bisexuality among many GE fans, a few MP fans repeatedly emphasized the rumors to others that the father of Muse's son was a gay man (daisyyvonne 2011). They also explained that Muse was possibly a "pure" lesbian who gave birth to a child with a gay man to "cover up her lesbian identity" or because she "wanted a child in her life" or to "fill up her emotional emptiness" (sunshisunshi 2012b). In particular, SMILE-VIVI, as an MP fan, said that it was possible for Muse to exploit her lesbian romance with Erichsen for "boosting her own career." Nonetheless, even if this was the case, it would be a "double-win" (*shuangying*) situation for the two because there was finally a stable, perfect family with an heir for Erichsen (2012d). However, in response to this idea of Erichsen building a wholesome family, several CP fans also asserted that she could have children with McNeil as well, as McNeil was still young and thus might have a perfect reproductive capability (weiduoliyademimi 2011b). In contrast, with McNeil's rumored past as a drug addict, alcoholic, and cheater to Erichsen with another Australian model Ruby Rose, one MP fan even commented that McNeil cannot win Erichsen's heart and does not even deserve to be a mistress of Erichsen's (dreamland88 2011b). These heated debates between the two fan groups lasted over a year and eventually caused several waves of fan hostilities in 2012. To mediate the growing internal factionalism, the discussion board administrator forbade many senior GE fans from viewing and posting, and deleted their previous posts.

The lesbian marriage and family imagined within these romanticized global scenes, though subjected to limited social pressure and legal constraint, are often deemed realizable on the premise that the qualified femme in a stable lesbian relationship should simultaneously be a "permanent" lesbian, a socially responsible and well-behaved person with mature personalities and social achievements, and someone who can perform her role as a good wife and mother in the lesbian family. More importantly, as stressed in the gossip, she should be able to produce heirs and therefore help the tomboy build a wholesome family. Here, one finds irony in the extent to which this conspicuous expression of "close-to-normal" mentality is undergirded by the vestiges of misogyny and biphobia ingrained in mainstream heteronormative cultures.

These fan sentiments of misogyny, biphobia, and related discriminations, hierarchies, and hostility widely exist in lesbian communities worldwide, especially the ones dismissing

FEMINIST RECEPTION STUDIES IN A POST-AUDIENCE AGE

(bisexual) femmes on the grounds of their heterosexual histories (Mary Bradford 2004; Hemmings 1998). Particularly, Engebretsen (2014) finds that an intrinsic gendered hierarchy shaped by heteronormative ideals persists in Chinese lesbian cultures in which traditionally feminine femmes (some of whom are bisexual) are usually believed to be lacking in perseverance, less committed, and more ready to give up on long-term lesbian relationships in favor of men (53).

Nevertheless, although discriminatory, the fans' efforts to search for alternative forms of imaginable lesbian romance in their Western imaginaries can also be construed as a strategy of queer reflection on the two hegemonic gendered systems—heterosexual marriage and patriarchal family—in mainstream Chinese society. In the 1990s Harriet Evans described the dominant heterosexual marriage model in post-Mao Chinese society in this way:

> The priority the dominant discourse gives to maintaining monogamous marriage as the site and pivot of all sexual activity and experience is overriding. This leaves no discursive space for women—or men—to choose difference, whether this means simply not marrying, having a lover outside marriage, or rejecting heterosexuality. In fact, it leaves no alternative for representations of a women's sexual fulfillment except in the subject positions identified by the status of wife and mother. (1997, 212)

Even in today's China, where the visibility of Chinese lesbians (and other queer groups) and their possibility of survival have greatly increased, "[m]arriage is [still] a rite to adulthood" (Lucetta Y. L. Kam 2010, 91). Meanwhile, the abilities of Chinese people—especially adult women—to get married and have children "are socially seen to be evidence of one's value in society and one's physical or psychological well-being" (Lucetta Y. L. Kam 2006, 92).

Furthermore, family (*jia*) has long been a major theme in Chinese queer cultures (Rofel 2007, 100). As Chris Berry finds, engaging in non-normative genders and sexualities does not necessarily mean a clear separation from the lived and conceptual constructions of family; instead, it might appear to "interfer[e] with the ability to perform one's role in the family" (2001, 215). Indeed, the notion of family in the Chinese context, though signifying a hegemonic dominant force, is inherently a fluid ideological construction that can be creatively rearticulated and compensated by and within queer relationships and thus proffers alternative opportunities and models of queer living (Engebretsen 2014, 59). The imagination of an alternative lesbian family model here developed on the basis of a possibly internalized but conscious choice to reconcile with dominant Chinese hetero-patriarchal expectations for women to perform "the combined role of 'good' daughter, wife, and mother" (Engebretsen 2014, 18). Many parts of the gossip, although recasting diverse normative elements of "innate femininity, marriage and motherhood" (Lisa Rofel 1999, 217) for adult women, also create possible spaces for the coexistence of non-heterosexual intimacies and traditionally patriarchal familial-marital structures.

For example, certain queer forms of family suggested in the gossip, such as the one through which gays and lesbians raise children together to create alternative kinship relations and thus build a homonormative family, can be read as a fan strategy to neutralize Muse's stigmatized heterosexual past. As implied in some fans' comments, this queer family model might also have opened up certain spaces for Muse's lesbian subjectivity. Also, SMILE-VIVI's "double-win" interpretation allowed the femme subject to "compensate" her "abnormal" lesbian relationship with a tomboy by bringing a male heir to the tomboy's family to form a queerly normalized family and thus to continue a pseudo-patriarchal family line. Meanwhile, this "double-win" model also enables the tomboy who is unable to form this kind of queer family with gay men or to produce an heir with males to "compensate" for their "deficiencies" by helping the career of her femme (in Muse's case, as a previously unknown model, her romance with Erichsen gained her a lot of media attention) in exchange for an alternative, wholesome, lesbian "family." Undoubtedly, this idea also significantly draws on Chinese heteronormative and patrilineal family structures. Yet, these "close-to-normal" imaginative moments in the gossip disclosed the fans' aspirations for imaginable lesbian marital-familial relations. The fans used their queerly normalized imaginaries of Erichsen's lesbianism as a platform to adapt lesbian gender roles, sexualities, and queer relationships—often deemed as undesirable, unsustainable, and less recognizable in mainstream Chinese society—into a variety of likely forms of queer female intimacies that are "proximate" to but not "the other of" Chinese traditional-patriarchal family and marriage (Fran Martin 2003, 182).

Conclusion

The universalizing Euro-American conception of lesbianism as *intrinsically* non-heteronormative and anti-hegemonic has long been criticized for its epistemic bias in that it treats sexual globalization as a form of Westernization and dismisses the constitutive force of local conditions and lived experiences. Building on this critique of the global gay model, this article uses a case study of transcultural Chinese fan practices to exemplify how non-Western queer subjects imaginatively negotiate with both local normative expectations of women's social roles and global homonormative popular culture. My account of GE fans' responses to Erichsen's queer images shows how the fans reflect—sometimes normatively—on the exploitation and manipulation of queer women's lives in both local and global public cultures. My discussion of the Chinese-specific "close-to-hetero-patriarchal" logic embedded in the fans' construction of Erichsen's tomboy sexuality and lesbian relationships also highlights the paradoxes of these queerly normalized transcultural lesbian imaginaries. I therefore highlight that these "normalizing" fan practices and discourses not only are circumscribed by the local Chinese traditional-patriarchal regulation of women's familial-marital roles, but also parodies that very same regulation. In this sense, this queer normalization reflected in the GE gossip both acknowledges and flirts with what mainstream public cultures define as impossible and invisible.

Notes

1. GE fandom is available at: http://bbs.sfile2012.com/
2. Although GE was Western-focused, threads devoted to queer readings of Chinese-speaking female celebrities could still be found. Most of these threads and posts did not attract much attention. Some posts and threads were even quickly deleted by the administrators to avoid further internal disputes or external "troubles." This tendency can be often found in online Chinese queer fandoms and explained as Chinese fans' tactics to protecting Chinese idols or as evidence of some Chinese fans' negative attitudes or even discrimination toward non-heterosexuality in the offline, Chinese world.
3. The lesbian-themed discussion board is available at: http://bbs.sfile2012.com/forumdisplay.php?fid=52&page=1&filter=type&typeid=308
4. The detailed GE survey results can be accessed from: http://bbs.sfile2012.com/viewthread.php?tid=24,296&extra=page%3D2%26amp%3Bfilter%3Dtype%26amp%3Btypeid%3D308, http://bbs.sfile2012.com/viewthread.php?tid=62,152&extra=page%3D1%26amp%3Bfilter%3Dtype%26amp%3Btypeid%3D308, and http://bbs.sfile2012.com/viewthread.php?tid=334895&extra=page%3D1

5. Erichsen stepped down from the catwalk in 2012 and has received low media exposure since then. GE fans' gossip devoted to her gradually died down after 2012 due to her rare public exposure.

6. The earliest GE thread devoted to Erichsen was started in September 2007 and obtained more than 12,504 entries. It is available at: http://bbs.sfile2012.com/viewthread.php?tid= 164,768&highlight=freja. In October 2008, the discussion board moderator terminated the posting function of the first thread due to its quota overflow for each thread in GE and started a second thread for queering Erichsen, which is available at: http://bbs.sfile2012.com/viewthread. php?tid=240263&highlight=freja. When the second thread obtained over 13,800 entries in August 2011, again exceeding its posting quota, a third thread was created for her. It is available at: http://bbs.sfile2012.com/viewthread.php?tid=346706&extra=&highlight=freja&page=1. By February 2015, the third thread had received 2,500 entries and had been viewed more than 110,300 times.

7. GL is an Asian subculture narrating stories about young female homoeroticism.

8. The remade images were later deleted by the GE administrator for their explicit homoeroticization of Erichsen, which stirred up controversies in some English-speaking fan sites.

9. Adapted from a well-known gay fiction by Wang Xiaobo, *East Palace, West Palace* is a famous Chinese gay film directed by Yuan Zhang in 1996. The GE fans used this phrase here to playfully imply the homoerotic feature of the relationships between these models.

Disclosure statement

No potential conflict of interest was reported by the author.

References

Adamson, Thomas. 2013. "Karl Lagerfeld supports gay marriage in lesbian couture." *Huffington Post*, January 22. http://www.huffingtonpost.com/2013/01/22/karl-lagerfeld-gay-marriage-lesbian-couture-_n_2525999.html

Berry, Chris. 2001. "Asian Values, Family Values: Film, Video, and Lesbian and Gay Identities." *Journal of Homosexuality* 40 (3–4): 211–231.

bibobibo. 2011. "Freja Beha Erichsen—The Rebel." *The L Word board*, June 20. http://bbs.sfile2012.com/viewthread.php?tid=240263&extra=&highlight=freja&page=537

Bradford, Mary. 2004. "The Bisexual Experience." *Journal of Bisexuality* 4 (1–2): 7–23.

bundchen. 2007a. "Freja Beha Erichsen—The Rebel." *The L Word board*, November 14. http://bbs.sfile2012.com/viewthread.php?tid=164768&extra=&highlight=freja&page=37

bundchen. 2007b. "Freja Beha Erichsen—The Rebel." *The L Word board*, November 14. http://bbs.sfile2012.com/viewthread.php?tid=164768&extra=&highlight=freja&page=37

Butler, Judith. 1990. *Gender Trouble*. New York: Routledge.

Champagne, John, and Elayne Tobin. 1997. "'She's Right Behind You': Gossip, Innuendo, and Rumour in the (De)Formation of Gay and Lesbian Studies." In *The Gay' 90s*, edited by Carol Siegel, Thomas Foster, and Ellen E. Berry, 51–82. New York: New York University Press.

Chao, Shi-Yan. 2010. "Coming out of The Box, Marching as Dykes." In *The New Chinese Documentary Film Movement*, edited by Lisa Rofel, Lu Xinyu, and Chris Berry, 77–95. Hong Kong: Hong Kong University Press.

daisyyvonne. 2011. "Freja Beha Erichsen: I Don't Move Unless I Have to." *The L Word board*, December 28. http://bbs.sfile2012.com/viewthread.php?tid=346706&extra=&highlight=freja&page=40

Dove-Viebahn, Aviva. 2007. "Fashionably Femme: Lesbian Visibility, Style, and Politics in *The L Word*." In *Queer Popular Culture*, edited by Thomas Peele, 71–83. New York: Palgrave MacMillan.

dr_momo. 2012a. "Freja Beha Erichsen: I Don't Move Unless I Have to." *The L Word board*, January 30. http://bbs.sfile2012.com/viewthread.php?tid=346706&extra=&highlight=freja&page=54

dr_momo. 2012b. "Freja Beha Erichsen: I Don't Move Unless I Have to." *The L Word board*, April 3. http://bbs.sfile2012.com/viewthread.php?tid=346706&extra=&highlight=freja&page=70

dr_momo. 2012c. "Freja Beha Erichsen: I Don't Move Unless I Have to." *The L Word board*, April 3. http://bbs.sfile2012.com/viewthread.php?tid=346706&extra=&highlight=freja&page=70

dreamland88. 2011a. "Freja Beha Erichsen—The Rebel." *The L Word board*, June 12. http://bbs.sfile2012.com/viewthread.php?tid=240263&extra=&highlight=freja&page=531

dreamland88. 2011b. "Freja Beha Erichsen—The Rebel." *The L Word board*, July 8. http://bbs.sfile2012.com/viewthread.php?tid=240263&extra=&highlight=freja&page=543

dreamland88. 2011c. "Freja Beha Erichsen—The Rebel." *The L Word board*, August 1. http://bbs.sfile2012.com/viewthread.php?tid=240263&extra=&highlight=freja&page=553

East Palace, West Palace. 1996. Directed by Yuan Zhang. China: Fortissimo Films.

Engebretsen, Elisabeth. 2014. *Queer Women in Urban China: An Ethnography*. New York: Routledge.

Evans, Harriet. 1997. *Women and Sexuality in China*. Oxford, UK: Polity Press.

Fiske, John. 1996. *Media Matters*. Minneapolis, MN: University of Minnesota Press.

Fiveandtaty. 2011a. "Freja Beha Erichsen—The Rebel." *The L Word board*, August 3. http://bbs.sfile2012.com/viewthread.php?tid=240263&extra=&highlight=freja&page=554

Fiveandtaty. 2011b. "Freja Beha Erichsen: I Don't Move Unless I Have to." *The L Word board*, November 8. http://bbs.sfile2012.com/viewthread.php?tid=346706&extra=&highlight=freja&page=30

Foucault, Michel. 1982. "The Subject and Power." In *Michel Foucault: Beyond Structuralism and Hermeneutics*, edited by Hubert L. Dreyfus, and Paul Rabinow, 208–226. Chicago, IL: The University of Chicago Press.

Gamson, Joshua. 1994. *Claims to Fame: Celebrity in Contemporary America*. Berkeley: University of California Press.

Georgakopoulou, Alexandra, and Dionysis Goutsos. 2004. *Discourse Analysis*. Edinburgh: Edinburgh University Press.

Halberstam, Judith. 1998. *Female Masculinity*. Durham, NC: Duke University Press.

Hemmings, Clare. 1998. "Waiting for No Man." In *Butch/Femme: Inside Lesbian Gender*, edited by Sully Munt, 90–100. Washington: Cassell.

Hermes, Joke. 1999. "Media Figures in Identity Construction." In *Rethinking the Media Audience*, edited by Pertti Alasuutari, 69–85. Thousand Oaks, CA: Sage Publications.

Hinsch, Bret. 1990. *Passions of the Cut Sleeve*. Los Angeles, CA: University of California Press.

hot1. 2011a. "Freja Beha Erichsen—The Rebel." *The L Word board*, January 20. http://bbs.sfile2012.com/viewthread.php?tid=240263&extra=&highlight=freja&page=491

hot1. 2011b. "Freja Beha Erichsen—The Rebel." *The L Word board*, April 5. http://bbs.sfile2012.com/viewthread.php?tid=240263&extra=&highlight=freja&page=511

hot1. 2011c. "Freja Beha Erichsen—The Rebel." *The L Word board*, May 18. http://bbs.sfile2012.com/viewthread.php?tid=240263&extra=&highlight=freja&page=525

hot1. 2011d. "Freja Beha Erichsen—The Rebel." *The L Word board*, June 24. http://bbs.sfile2012.com/viewthread.php?tid=240263&extra=&highlight=freja&page=540

hot1. 2011e. "Freja Beha Erichsen: I Don't Move Unless I Have to." *The L Word board*, November 3. http://bbs.sfile2012.com/viewthread.php?tid=346706&extra=&highlight=freja&page=28

JoePortard. 2011a. "Freja Beha Erichsen—The Rebel." *The L Word board*, January 20. http://bbs.sfile2012.com/viewthread.php?tid=240263&extra=&highlight=freja&page=491

JoePortard. 2011b. "Freja Beha Erichsen—The Rebel." *The L Word board*, January 22. http://bbs.sfile2012.com/viewthread.php?tid=240263&extra=&highlight=freja&page=492

JoePortard. 2011c. "Freja Beha Erichsen—The Rebel." *The L Word board*, June 14. http://bbs.sfile2012.com/viewthread.php?tid=240263&extra=&highlight=freja&page=532

kal. 2011. "Freja Beha Erichsen—The Rebel." *The L Word board*, January 20. http://bbs.sfile2012.com/viewthread.php?tid=240263&extra=&highlight=freja&page=491

Kam, Lucetta Y. L. 2006. "Noras on the Road: Family and Marriage of Lesbian Women in Shanghai." *Journal of Lesbian Studies* 10 (3–4): 87–103.

Kam, Lucetta Y. L. 2010. "Opening Up Marriage." In *As normal as possible*, edited by Ching Yau, 87–102. Hong Kong: Hong Kong University Press.

Kam, Lucetta Y. L. 2013. *Female Tongzhi Communities and Politics in Urban China*. Hong Kong: Hong Kong University Press.

Kam, Lucetta Y. L. 2014. "Desiring T, Desiring Self." *Journal of Lesbian Studies* 18 (3): 252–265.

Kong Travis, S. K. 2011. *Chinese Male Homosexualities: Memba, Tongzhi and Golden Boy*. New York: Routledge.

kt12117. 2011a. "Freja Beha Erichsen: I Don't Move Unless I Have to." *The L Word board*, September 17. http://bbs.sfile2012.com/viewthread.php?tid=346706&extra=&highlight=freja&page=12

kt12117. 2011b. "Freja Beha Erichsen: I Don't Move Unless I Have to." *The L Word board*, September 24. http://bbs.sfile2012.com/viewthread.php?tid=346706&extra=&highlight=freja&page=13

Leung, Helen. 2008. *Undercurrents*. Vancouver: University of British Columbia Press.

Liu, Jen-peng, and Naifei Ding. 2005. "Reticent Poetics, Queer Politics." *Inter-Asia Cultural Studies* 6 (1): 30–55.

logmei1009log. 2011. "Freja Beha Erichsen—The Rebel." *The L Word board*, July 11. http://bbs.sfile2012.com/viewthread.php?tid=240263&extra=&highlight=freja&page=545.

lois323. 2011. "Freja Beha Erichsen: I Don't Move Unless I Have to." *The L Word board*, November 3. http://bbs.sfile2012.com/viewthread.php?tid=346706&extra=&highlight=freja&page=28

Lu, Shen, and Katie Hunt. 2015. "China: Student Sues over Textbooks that 'Demonize' Gays and Lesbians." *CNN*, August 20. http://edition.cnn.com/2015/08/19/asia/china-lesbian-student-court-case/

Marshall, David. 1997. *Celebrity and Power: Fame in Contemporary Culture*. Minneapolis, MN: University of Minnesota Press.

Martin, Fran. 2003. *Situating Sexualities*. Hong Kong: Hong Kong University Press.

Martin, Fran. 2010. *Backward Glances: Contemporary Chinese Cultures and the Female Homoerotic Imaginary*. Durham, NC: Duke University Press.

Martin, Fran. 2011. "Getting over It: Thinking beyond the Hetero(genizing)/Homo(genizing) Divide in Transnational Sexuality Studies." *English Language Notes* 49 (1): 117–123.

Martin, Fran. 2015. "Queer Pop Culture in the Sinophone Mediasphere." Paper presented at the Inter-Asia Cultural Studies Conference, Surabaya, Indonesia, August 7–9.

Meyers, Erin. 2010. "Gossip Talk and Online Community: Celebrity Gossip Blogs and Their Audiences." PhD diss. University of Massachusetts-Amherst.

mingmingmingyu. 2012. "Freja Beha Erichsen: I Don't Move Unless I Have to." *The L Word Board*, March 25. http://bbs.sfile2012.com/viewthread.php?tid=346706&extra=&highlight=freja&page=68

neutrogena. 2007. "Freja Beha Erichsen—The Rebel." *The L Word board*, November 14. http://bbs.sfile2012.com/viewthread.php?tid=164768&extra=&highlight=freja&page=37

Remember Now. 2010. Directed by Karl Lagerfeld. France: Chanel.

Rofel, Lisa. 1999. *Other Modernities: Gendered Yearnings in China after Socialism*. Berkeley: University of California Press.

Rofel, Lisa. 2007. *Desiring China*. Durham, NC: Duke University Press.

Rojek, Chris. 2001. *Celebrity*. London: Reaktion Books.

samdream. 2011. "Freja Beha Erichsen: I Don't Move Unless I Have to." *The L Word Board*, September 25. http://bbs.sfile2012.com/viewthread.php?tid=346706&extra=&highlight=freja&page=13

Sang, Tze-lan. 2003. *The Emerging Lesbian*. Chicago, IL: The University of Chicago Press.

sea000mus. 2011. "Freja Beha Erichsen—The Rebel." *The L Word board*, January 25. http://bbs.sfile2012.com/viewthread.php?tid=240263&extra=&highlight=freja&page=492

sea000mus. 2012a. "Freja Beha Erichsen: I Don't Move Unless I Have to." *The L Word board*, January 30. http://bbs.sfile2012.com/viewthread.php?tid=346706&extra=&highlight=freja&page=54

sea000mus. 2012b. "Freja Beha Erichsen: I Don't Move Unless I Have to." *The L Word Board*, January 30. http://bbs.sfile2012.com/viewthread.php?tid=346706&extra=&highlight=freja&page=54

Shi, Liang. 2015. *Chinese Lesbian Cinema*. Lanham, ML: Lexington.

shitchild. 2011. "Freja Beha Erichsen—The Rebel." *The L Word board*, June 24. http://bbs.sfile2012.com/viewthread.php?tid=240263&extra=&highlight=freja&page=540

SMILE-VIVI. 2012a. "Freja Beha Erichsen: I Don't Move Unless I Have to." *The L Word board*, January 29. http://bbs.sfile2012.com/viewthread.php?tid=346706&extra=&highlight=freja&page=53

SMILE-VIVI. 2012b. "Freja Beha Erichsen: I Don't Move Unless I Have to." *The L Word board*, January 30. http://bbs.sfile2012.com/viewthread.php?tid=346706&extra=&highlight=freja&page=54

SMILE-VIVI. 2012c. "Freja Beha Erichsen: I Don't Move Unless I Have to." *The L Word board*, January 30. http://bbs.sfile2012.com/viewthread.php?tid=346706&extra=&highlight=freja&page=54

SMILE-VIVI. 2012d. "Freja Beha Erichsen: I Don't Move Unless I Have to." *The L Word board*, January 30. http://bbs.sfile2012.com/viewthread.php?tid=346706&extra=&highlight=freja&page=54

sousou2. 2011a. "Freja Beha Erichsen—The Rebel." *The L Word board*, July 10. http://bbs.sfile2012.com/viewthread.php?tid=240263&extra=&highlight=freja&page=544

sousou2. 2011b. "Freja Beha Erichsen—The Rebel." *The L Word board*, July 18. http://bbs.sfile2012.com/viewthread.php?tid=240263&extra=&highlight=freja&page=547

sousou2. 2011c. "Freja Beha Erichsen: I Don't Move Unless I Have to." *The L Word board*, October 23. http://bbs.sfile2012.com/viewthread.php?tid=346706&extra=&highlight=freja&page=24

sunshisunshi. 2012a. "Freja Beha Erichsen: I Don't Move Unless I Have to." *The L Word board*, January 30. http://bbs.sfile2012.com/viewthread.php?tid=346706&extra=&highlight=freja&page=54

sunshisunshi. 2012b. "Freja Beha Erichsen: I Don't Move Unless I Have to." *The L Word board*, January 30. http://bbs.sfile2012.com/viewthread.php?tid=346706&extra=&highlight=freja&page=54

The Tale of the Fairy. 2011. Directed by Karl Lagerfeld. France: Chanel.

Walker, Danny. 2015. "Documentary Claims to Expose China's Gay Shock Therapy that Looks for 'Homosexuality Cure.'" *Mirror*, October 9. http://www.mirror.co.uk/tv/tv-news/documentary-claims-expose-chinas-gay-6606387

weiduoliyademimi. 2011a. "Freja Beha Erichsen—The Rebel." *The L Word board*, January 24. http://bbs.sfile2012.com/viewthread.php?tid=240263&extra=&highlight=freja&page=492

weiduoliyademimi. 2011b. "Freja Beha Erichsen—The Rebel." *The L Word board*, March 16. http://bbs.sfile2012.com/viewthread.php?tid=240263&extra=&highlight=freja&page=502

weiduoliyademimi. 2011c. "Freja Beha Erichsen—The Rebel." *The L Word board*, May 18. http://bbs.sfile2012.com/viewthread.php?tid=240263&extra=&highlight=freja&page=525

weiduoliyademimi. 2011d. "Freja Beha Erichsen—The Rebel." *The L Word board*, July 12. http://bbs.sfile2012.com/viewthread.php?tid=240263&extra=&highlight=freja&page=545

weiduoliyademimi. 2011e. "Freja Beha Erichsen: I Don't Move Unless I Have to." *The L Word board*, October 22. http://bbs.sfile2012.com/viewthread.php?tid=346706&extra=&highlight=freja&page=24

Xiao, Hui Faye. 2012. "Androgynous Beauty, Virtual Sisterhood: Stardom, Fandom, and Chinese Talent Shows under Globalization." In *Super Girls, Gangstas, Freeters, and Xenomaniacs*, edited by Susan Dewey, and Karen J. Brison, 103–124. Syracuse, New York: Syracuse University Press.

Y1017. 2011. "Freja Beha Erichsen—The Rebel." *The L Word board*, March 14. http://bbs.sfile2012.com/viewthread.php?tid=240263&extra=&highlight=freja&page=500

Yau, Ching. 2010. "Dreaming of Normal While Sleeping with Impossible: Introduction." In *As Normal as Possible*, edited by Ching Yau, 1–14. Hong Kong: Hong Kong University Press.

Zimmerman, Bonnie. 1992. "Lesbians like This and That: Some Notes on Lesbian Criticism for the Nineties." In *New Lesbian Criticism: Literary and Cultural Readings*, edited by Sally Munt, 1–15. New York: Columbia University Press.

zoenoah. 2007a. "Freja Beha Erichsen—The Rebel." *The L Word board*, October 18. http://bbs.sfile2012.com/viewthread.php?tid=164768&extra=&highlight=freja&page=18

zoenoah. 2007b. "Freja Beha Erichsen—The Rebel." *The L Word board*, November 14. http://bbs.sfile2012.com/viewthread.php?tid=164768&extra=&highlight=freja&page=37

zonlomo4. 2011. "Freja Beha Erichsen—The Rebel." *The L Word board*, May 6. http://bbs.sfile2012.com/viewthread.php?tid=240263&extra=&highlight=freja&page=521

Leave a comment: mommyblogs and the everyday struggle to reclaim parenthood

Linda Steiner and Carolyn Bronstein

ABSTRACT

"Mommyblogs" are significant for feminist media theory, given how these give mothers a public venue to voice their experiences and anxieties at a stage of life that often generates new feminist insight. Whereas previous generations of mothers relied on interpersonal communication and books authored by professional experts, contemporary mothers are more likely to seek parenting information and offer advice by reading and responding to blogs. These media texts are also bases of communal support, blurring older theories of audience "reception" and complicating notions of expertise, authority, and power. Analysis of comments about two controversies—one involving the measles vaccination, the other about so-called free-range parenting—posted to the *New York Times Motherlode* blog shows that parenting blogs enable audience members—not only women but also men—to debate parenting decisions that result from neoliberal imperatives. Commenters both endorse neoliberal parenting, framing it as an exercise in good decision-making and risk management that yields positive outcomes, and contest it, arguing that parenting must contribute to social and collective justice. The audience thereby discursively participates in an everyday form of activism that enables citizens to help shape the terms of public debate.

Introduction

Shifts in the expectations for and demands of mothering are continuing to command attention, especially in the context of contemporary neoliberalism, that is, policies that cultivate individualism, competition, acquisition, and entrepreneurialism. Acknowledging that its tenets are not uniformly accepted, Jeremy Gilbert (2013) highlights the basic elements of neoliberal ideology: privatization of public assets, contraction and centralization of democratic institutions, restrictions on labor organization, labor market deregulation, and active encouragement of competition and entrepreneurship across the public and commercial sectors. More specifically, Angela McRobbie (2013) points out that neoliberalism rejects, both ideologically and practically, key demands of earlier generations of mothers and feminists, such as mandatory paid family leave, collectivist and state-supported childcare, and wages for housework. Neoliberalism and mothering may at first glance seem irreconcilable for how they pit individual interests against social welfare. Yet successful mothers are increasingly depicted as entrepreneurial subjects who find their own solutions to problems of domestic labor and childcare, typically relying on private economic assets. "Good mothers" these days are typically upper middle-class successful professionals with the means to raise their children independently of any state support, including public schools.

Contemporary neoliberalism has so neatly accommodated feminism and the women's movement that recognizing their inherent conflicts of interest is difficult. Shani Orgad and Sara De Benedictis (2015) point out the "intensifying entanglement" of contemporary mothering and neoliberalism (2015, 420). As a result, "successful femininities increasingly have come to be defined as neoliberal identities, marking women as individualized, autonomous, freely choosing, self-monitoring and self-disciplining subjects" (2015, 418–419). This is especially evident in public discourse around motherhood, which has been recast in a neoliberal framework as a competitive exercise in highly personalized decision-making, material consumption, and personal expenditure. McRobbie (2013) argues that working mothers, previously castigated as insufficiently dedicated to their children, are no longer vilified if they perform according to neoliberalism's demands. Indeed, they are celebrated if they embrace highly restrictive, gendered self-management routines (working but also working out) such that they are simultaneously sexually attractive, economically productive, and endlessly nurturing. Feminism has been rehabilitated, McRobbie argues, albeit at the cost of accepting an ethos of competitive individualism. Stay-at-home, middle-class mothers are also accounted for in the neoliberal framework: they must be responsible household managers, efficiently deploying available resources to greatest advantage, and strategically figuring out how to protect children from excessive risk while maximizing their potential for success and even competitive edge.

Sharon Hays (1996, 8) introduced the term "intensive mothering" to describe the "emotionally absorbing, labor-intensive, and financially expensive" undertaking that motherhood had become by the mid-1990s. Many scholars agree that intensive mothering is the "ascendant ideology in North America" (Karen Christopher 2012, 75). Susan Douglas and Meredith Michaels (2004) similarly emphasize how the impossible and contradictory standards of the "new momism" keep women striving for unreachable goals, forcing mothers to swing between the "Madonna–whore poles of perfect and failed motherhood" (27).

The convergence of discourses around intensive parenting, neoliberalism, and risk provides the basis for our consideration of posts and reader comments on a popular *New York Times* website, *Motherlode*/Adventures in Parenting.[1] With all the scholarly attention to personal mommy bloggers (e.g., Lori Kido-Lopez 2009), the importance of communal-structured online parenting spaces such as *Motherlode* has not been fully explored. *Motherlode* in particular is the preeminent parenting site, giving diverse mothers a public venue to share their experiences and anxieties at a stage of life—when their children's lives and futures seem to be at stake—that often generates a kind of practical everyday feminism and new feminist insights.[2] We focus on two controversies prominent in 2015 that turned on fairly routine choices that parents make about risk: vaccination and "free-range" parenting. Audience members negotiated questions of parenting style, such as whether to vaccinate or not, in highly complex ways, illustrating both internalization and acceptance of intensive parenting norms and, less frequently, a commitment to contesting them. Katherine Sender (2015) demonstrated that reality television uses surveillance narratives to encourage citizens to self-police and manage themselves in ways that are compatible with neoliberal politics. Do parenting blogs perform similar functions? Indeed, like reality television stars who invite the world to judge their bodies, relationships, and talents, *Motherlode* commenters open their family lives up for comparison and critique. Some are praised for their parenting decisions. Others are shamed and directed to change.

The vaccination question turned on the debate about the safety or risk of childhood vaccination for measles, long-simmering after a British physician linked—in a fraudulent, now-retracted 1998 research article—the childhood measles–mumps–rubella (MMR) vaccines to autism. Rates of delayed or incomplete childhood vaccination increased after *The Lancet* publication and celebrities' highly publicized criticisms of vaccination and refusal to vaccinate their children. Between December 2014 and March 2015, California reported 133 confirmed cases of measles, linked to visitors to Disneyland; at least half of the victims had not been vaccinated. Physicians maintain that MMR is 95 percent effective in preventing measles, which is contagious and can lead to serious, permanent, and even fatal effects. When at least 96 percent of a population is vaccinated against measles, then even vulnerable individuals who cannot be vaccinated because of allergies or severe medical problems are protected. In the US, "the herd protection" no longer exists because so many "anti-vaxer" parents have decided against routine vaccination.

The second issue turned on a parenting philosophy known as "free-range parenting," a "commonsense" counterpoint to overbearing, overprotective "helicopter" parenting. Lenore Skenazy, a blogger and founder of the Free Range Kids Movement, wrote a 2008 *New York Sun* column about allowing her nine-year-old son to ride the New York subway alone. Parents both condemned and praised her parenting methods:

> Half the people I've told this episode to now want to turn me in for child abuse. As if keeping kids under lock and key … and surveillance is the right way to rear kids. It's not. It's debilitating—for us and for them. (Lenore Skenazy 2008)

On her Free-Range Kids website, Skenazy maintains: "Our kids are safer than we think, and more competent, too. They deserve a chance to stretch and grow and do what we did—stay out till the street lights come on" (*Freerangekids.com*). Over the years, this parenting style has attracted adherents and attention, including a 2009 *WebMD* article. The real publicity came, however, in 2015 when two self-declared free-range parents were investigated for suspicion of child neglect after neighbors reported them for allowing their children to walk home alone from a park. The park was located about a mile away from their suburban Maryland home. The ten-year-old boy and his six-year-old sister were halfway home when, alerted by an onlooker, the police picked them up. Police officers subsequently questioned parents Danielle and Alexander Meitiv, who insisted that they had carefully prepared their children for that walk. This case brought enormous national and international print and broadcast publicity. *The Huffington Post*, for example, ran two dozen related columns between January 2015 and July 2016. Ironically, days before the Meitivs were investigated, a rider to a federal education bill was signed into law stipulating that parental permission was all that was needed to allow an unaccompanied child to walk or bicycle to and from school.

Mothers and the roles of blogs

Always crucial to projects in gender ideology, media aimed at women have long addressed standards of mothering. Becoming a parent is often highly stressful, bringing psychological, physical, and social pressures, especially for mothers. With child-rearing still largely associated with women (Kim Akass 2012), mothers are particularly active information-seekers. Whereas previous generations of mothers relied on advice books as well as friends, pediatricians, and family (and family members were often nearby), mothers today increasingly turn to parenting blogs. Especially for new mothers, frequent blogging provides both a distraction and a sense of connection to family and friends, which predicts maternal well-being (Brandon McDaniel, Sarah Coyne, and Erin Holmes 2012).

Most mommyblogs are controlled by individual mothers who emphasize consumer advice.[3] These bloggers typically give advice about products, often on the basis of having received free products or samples. One study found that they frequently generate buzz about relevant businesses; and 93 percent of moms take into account fellow moms' reviews, feedback, and opinions when making any purchase (Amie Marse 2013). According to widely-cited market research, 14 percent of US mothers either blog about parenting or turn to blogs for advice; the average mommyblogger's household income is approximately $14,000 higher than for non-blogging moms. Industry observers note the significance: "The ascent of the Mommy Blogger has been rapid, and her wild popularity, power and influence cannot be ignored" (Scott Gulbransen 2012).

Many mommyblogs take a more personal approach to parenting, and authors typically share everyday stories of family life, such as teaching a child to walk or managing sibling jealousy. Aimée Morrison (2011) emphasizes the appeal of the intimate public of personal mommyblogging: it offers emotional release, given the direct emotional reciprocity among its readers and commenters, and a satisfying, coherent identity in which to contextualize personal experience. But even Morrison, herself a personal mommyblogger, notes that this format blunts the political force of its critique of contemporary womanhood by rigidly separating its intimate public from mainstream public culture and minimizing its visibility to a broader, outsider audience.

Institutionally-sponsored parenting blogs such as *Motherlode* (rebranded as *Well Family* in March 2016) play a different—and significant—role in that they provide diverse readers with structured spaces to work through complex issues.[4] Responding to sophisticated posts on such topics as school choice, learning differences, divorce, and gender orientation, *Motherlode* readers can actively support or conversely question and/or resist dominant parenting paradigms, endorse or challenge neoliberal arrangements. They can—and do—position themselves as experts regarding their own children or parenting in general. Both personal and organizational sites blur older theories of audience "reception" and complicate notions of expertise, authority, and power. The potential for blogs to enable parents to seriously and thoughtfully engage with one another, rather than passively consuming the media's mothering advice—typically "more an instruction manual on what suits society than what is best for our mothers and children" (Akass 2012, 138)—is evident on *Motherlode*.

New York Times writer Lisa Belkin founded *Motherlode* in 2008. Belkin's relationship to *Motherlode* is significant: her (2003) much publicized and controversial account of highly educated women who "opted out" of the work force when their children were born was widely criticized for stoking tensions between stay-at-home and working mothers, exacerbating maternal guilt, and validating sexist beliefs that women belong at home with their children (Akass 2012). Belkin herself "admitted" (her verb) that she left her previous *Times* job for the greater flexibility of the blog not because her children needed her but because she wanted an easier job. In 2011, KJ Dell'Antonia, a former prosecutor and prolific blogger who lives in New Hampshire with her family, took over as its lead writer and editor.

Blogs have evolved as an important source of support for mothers. This is especially significant in the era of the "mommy wars," manufactured conflicts that journalists have exploited since Jan Jarboe Russell's 1989 *Texas Monthly* essay "The Mommy War" about hostilities between working moms and stay-at-home moms. Toni Schindler Zimmerman, Jennifer T. Aberle, Jennifer L. Krafchick, and Ashley M. Harvey (2008) justifiably accused several popular US talk and reality television shows of emphasizing the mommy wars "to divert the dialogue away from real issues" such as affordable health care, childcare, gender and racial equality, and fathers' parenting roles (204). In one of the rare acknowledgements of journalists' role in hyping divisiveness, the *Washington Post* admitted: "The ballyhooed Mommy Wars exist mainly in the minds—and the marketing machines—of the media and publishing industry, which have been churning out mom vs. mom news flashes since … the 1950s" (E. J. Graff 2007). Free-range parenting advocate Skenazy says she never realized how much the media loves parenting controversies until she saw how journalists sought to pit her in high-visibility media battles against "helicopter" parents.[5]

Neoliberal parenting and managing risk

Neoliberalism's intensified focus on the private sector and endorsement of cuts in state-funded programs for children and families requires parents to fill in the gap, to take on responsibility for high-quality childcare, education, and health and welfare services. Intensive parents must therefore acquire detailed knowledge of what the experts consider proper child development and spend considerable time, energy, and money on education, childcare, and speech, behavioral, and occupational therapies. For example, this orientation is visible in debates about the risks associated with infant formula; breastfeeding has become "an ideologically infused moral discourse about what it means to be a 'good mother' in an advanced capitalist society" (Stephanie J. Knaak 2010, 345). Intensive mothering has come to dominate mothering ideals in the UK and US (Hays 1996; Glenda Wall 2001). Intensive mothering requires mothers—even if they work full-time—to take full responsibility for their children's physical and psychological health, and prioritize children's emotional and intellectual development (Mary Blair-Loy 2003; Hays 1996; Deirdre D. Johnston and Debra H. Swanson 2007).

Children, meanwhile, are increasingly represented as vulnerable and lacking self-control (Virginia Caputo 2007; Diane M. Hoffman 2010; Ellie Lee, Jan Macvarish, and Jennie Bristow 2010). As Frank Furedi (2008) notes, the threshold of "acceptable" risk has declined dramatically and the supposed stakes and ubiquitous dangers require increased parental surveillance and consultation with a battery of professional child experts (Knaak 2010). Potential risks to children and the risks attached to inadequate parenting figure prominently in neoliberal discourse. Susan Braedley and Meg Luxton (2010) observe that neoliberalism encourages *investment parenting*—pouring one's time, labor, and resources into children to ensure good market returns. Lee, Macvarish, and Bristow (2010, 294) note that the demands on contemporary parents "far outstrips demands placed on previous generations" and that this expansion has taken place alongside the growing notion that children are always "at risk." Reminiscent of stock market strategies, parents minimize risk while maximizing return on investment (in one's children). Liberal risk regimes emphasize knowledge of risk management and risk taking, with risk takers expected to be informed self-sufficient consumers and to see "all differences, and the inequalities that result from them ... as a matter of choice" (Richard V. Ericson, Aaron Doyle, and Dean Barry 2003, 1360).

Patricia Collins (1994, 59) notes that in oppressive contexts mothers realize that "individual survival, empowerment, and identity require group survival, empowerment, and identity, i.e., communal motherhood." But neoliberalism decimates this it-takes-a-village approach and emphasizes that children's success is best achieved through fierce competition and individual striving. Contemporary parents have become redefined as "risk managers" charged with protecting a precious commodity (Lee, Macvarish, and Bristow 2010). All parenting decisions, from how parents discipline their children to how they let them play outdoors, become contested and politicized as connected to measurable outcomes.

Neoliberal imperatives may dominate public discourse today, but they do not produce intensive parenting conformance across the board. New media technologies stimulate vigorous audience opposition. Many commenters use parenting blogs to decry the current parenting climate as stifling and damaging to children and parents alike, to resist hegemonic intensive discourses. Some individual parents compete in ways that are highly consistent with neoliberal values and that thereby disavow post-war ideas of collectivism, social welfare, and community. Others, however, contest the privileging of the individual child at the expense of a shared commitment to a more general good. By providing a space for discursive activism, these blogs function not only as important sources of information but also as bases of communal support. These online sites may be seen as moral battlefields in which every parenting decision is vulnerable to attack. But blogs also reinvigorate discussions about gender politics, underscoring how the challenges facing mothers could be framed in terms of social and collective justice (Nancy Fraser 2013).

Method

Internet field research methods regarding audience responses to the major posts and readers' interactions with one another formed the basis for our approach (Frances Shaw 2013). By investigating *Motherlode*, the leading parenting blog, we sought to understand the significance of everyday discursive politics for contemporary parents online. We analyzed all responses to all 2015 columns about two red-hot topics: MMR, after a measles outbreak traced to Disneyland and continuing vigorous opposition to the vaccination; and free-range parenting, in the wake of official investigation of self-proclaimed free-range parents. *Motherlode* ran three pieces about MMR, which of all vaccination issues drew the most number of responses.[6] Rachel Rabkin Peachman's January 21 post drew the highest number in two days. Dell'Antonia's January 29 piece drew 234 responses, nearly all of them within three days. A few days later, KJ Dell'Antonia's (2015c) "Want More Vaccinated Kids? End Religious and Personal Exemptions," with its less conciliatory tone, drew 353 comments. Dell'Antonia wrote two *Motherlode* pieces about the free range debate. Her first (2015a) column about arrests of the Meitivs drew 132 comments plus dozens of replies to individual commenters. Four months later, after the couple again ran into trouble with the state, her follow-up (2015b) drew 218 comments plus dozens of replies to individual commenters.

We read the responses several times to establish major themes and coding categories, and then re-read them closely several times, following Stuart Hall's (1975) advice for thick reading. After coding separately, and then working through the results together, we selected representative (and sometimes exceptional) quotes and examples. Commenters included hard-core supporters of *Motherlode* columnists, supporters who pushed the columnists' argument farther; opponents who sought to dismantle or discredit the original argument; and people who largely ignored the original column while responding to and interacting with other commenters. Commenters identified themselves as from all over the US (and occasionally outside), and many responded on both issues—and on other issues not studied here.[7]

Consistent with *Times* blog policy, *Motherlode* is moderated by its editor and professional staff, who ensure that all posted comments are respectful and refer directly to the subject in question (Andrew Rosenthal 2012). Dell'Antonia (2015d) wrote that she rejected comments that were inflammatory, name-calling, rude to fellow commenters, irrelevant, incoherent, or obscene. While "active moderation" slows and sometimes detracts from the conversation, Dell'Antonia acknowledged, it also enhances civil conversation and maintains a sense of community.[8] Comments from trolls seeking to disrupt and derail discussion were, for the most part, absent, a strategy that encourages *Motherlode* readers to share fully-formed opinions and honest perspectives, knowing that they may be subject to heated disagreement, but not personal vitriol.

Given the assumption that *Motherlode* serves primarily mothers and that fathers are active on the site to a lesser extent, we were particularly interested to analyze two occasions when fathers also responded to high-profile issues: vaccination and free-range parenting. We sought to understand how commenters challenged or reinforced hegemonic discourses about good mothers and intensive parenting through discursive interventions around those issues. It is not possible to determine the percentage of *Motherlode* comments by gender, parenting status, or profession. However, people tended to comment using what they claimed were their real (typically gendered) names, and posted photographs or selected avatars indicating gender. Using these guideposts and *Motherlode*'s decidedly serious space for public comment, we concluded that, at least regarding these issues, men, mostly fathers, were highly active as commenters. Indeed, the site's gender-inclusive renaming as *Well Family* indicates a changed understanding of modern family structures and fathers' increased involvement in parenting.

Vaccination

Neoliberalism's highly gendered double-edged sword came into focus with Disney's measles outbreak, since, if healthy children represent the outcome of good neoliberal mothering, then mothers can be blamed when their children are sick (Linda Blum 2007). As Jennifer A. Reich (2014) found, mothers who disobeyed state mandates for vaccinations saw themselves as equipped to weigh medical risks in the name of protecting their children. By focusing solely on their own children, per intensive mothering practices, they ignored both how their children benefit from others' immunity and how their choices undermine community health; each mother's insistence that her individual choice proved her maternal commitment replicated structural inequality. UK mothers likewise stressed the particularity of their child; they individualized or personalized risk, ignoring epidemiological data (Mike Poltorak, Melissa Leach, James Fairhead, and Jackie Cassell 2005). Medical professionals are increasingly urged to cultivate respect and trust among parents in order to boost vaccination rates (Deborah A. Gust, Natalie Darling, Allison Kennedy, and Ben Schwartz 2008). But vaccine resistance groups have a highly negative view of the leap of faith at the heart of trust, often regarding trust in others as a passive and easy option at odds with informed parenting (Pru Hobson-West 2007). Vaccine resisters' view of trust as itself a source of risk (Poltorak et al. 2005, 714) is consistent with neoliberal parenting: good parents do the research necessary to become well-informed on all topics and make choices that are best for their children.

The first of *Motherlode*'s major MMR columns in 2015, Rachel Rabkin Peachman's (2015) piece explained how the measles virus was eliminated in the US in 2000, thanks to a 99-percent effective vaccine. Peachman positioned herself as a mother and as a health journalist; in the latter context, she had spent years explaining the importance and safety of a vaccine against a disease that could cause encephalitis, pneumonia, blindness, deafness, permanent neurological disability, and even death. Dell'Antonia (2015b) wrote about a six-year-old California boy with leukemia who could not be vaccinated. His father asked the local school district to block unvaccinated children from attending school, because 7 percent of the student body was unvaccinated, thereby undermining herd immunity. The Marin County health officer refused, citing "everybody's right to freedom." Dell'Antonia sympathized with the parent and child: "Ultimately, the best solution for a child who is relying on the kindness—or herd immunity—of strangers lies in the hands of the strangers themselves." A few days later, Dell'Antonia (2015c) took a far less conciliatory tone, complaining that California enables "free riding" by letting families opt out. To boost vaccination rates, she insisted, "state legislatures need to end both religious and personal exemptions to the requirement that children be vaccinated in order to attend public schools." Dell'Antonia asserted that strengthening protection merely required imposing a strict vaccine requirement—without loopholes.

Style and language

Whether because *Motherlode* attracted more readers, more partisan readers, or the issues became more controversial, the MMR articles always drew hundreds of responses, and these numbers increased over time. MMR drew large numbers of posts noting flaws in claims that connected the vaccine to autism. It might be noted from the outset that the overwhelming number of commenters defended vaccines or, even more commonly, attacked the "anti-vaxers." The debate turned not on the benefits or downsides of MMR but on what methods were likely to be effective in convincing anti-vaxers, or, indeed, if anything would convince them. This could backfire, such as when Susan Marks (January 22, 2015), having claimed her pediatrician asked her not to tell others that her toddler had a seizure after getting an MMR, objected to the implication that only pro-vaxers want to protect children: "Sorry my child matters too." On February 3, Marks protested:

> This blog is so one sided and self-righteous. ... It is not a joke or a plot by earth is flat people. Get past your smugness and stop hectoring parents. I vaccinate my kids but if anything, hysterically angry blogs like this turn people off.

Moreover, the issue was parenting, not mothers per se. One exception was Banty AcidJazz, a very frequent "trusted commenter" (January 30, 2015) who said anti-vaxers claimed to be "more mother-bear than you." Banty AcidJazz also described them as "armed with the usual conspiracy-theory beliefs," suspicious of mainstream medical science and "the gub'mint." On February 6, 2015, Banty AcidJazz described the anti-vaxers as "out mother-bearing (don't YOU care about YOUR child like we do??) everyone else." Given the context, Vanessa (January 22, 2015) implied that anti-vaxers are mothers who grow hysterical when "their little darlings" get mildly ill. Of course, some posters identified as mothers. It was primarily mothers who reported that their children were MMR-injured.

The mothers and fathers who worried about MMR were a distinct minority and their posts drew few recommendations, but they were not shy about expressing their views. Tracy Steinbach (February 3, 2015) frequently debated, and directly criticized, people who questioned her account of how her two children each long ago suffered a vaccine-caused "acquired brain injury." Although pro-vaxers noted the effects on children in a variety of public places, a mother who refused to vaccinate her kids (Anna H, February 4, 2015) explained: "Since we are choosing to home school, that shouldn't bother anyone, should it? Freedom of choice. Let me make my choices, and you make yours." Al (February 5, 2015) insisted that parents claim religious exemption because that is the only way that they are not forced to do something that may cause "a terrible reaction."

Notably, although vaccination advocates regularly called themselves "pro-vax" (or "pro-vac"), the few posters against or suspicious of the MMR never called themselves "anti-vaxer," perhaps seeing it as a brusque term that trivialized beliefs formed after careful study and consideration. Me (January 22, 2015) said: "please don't call me an 'anti-vaxer,' you can call me fully informed consenter, or non-consenter." Banty AcidJazz (January 23, 2015), among many others, insisted that while anti-vaxers describe themselves as "fully informed non-consenter," "fully informed" meant believing misinformed websites. The most common assertion by pro-vax posters was that, as RLBS put it (January 22, 2015): "Anti-vaxers seem to think they know better than the medical community and years of indisputable evidence." Other frequent epithets were paranoid, stupid, dimwitted, selfish, and hysterical. They were also deemed anti-social, cruel, and arrogant. Promising to "call a spade a spade," Peter (January 22, 2015) said anti-vaxers "are bad parents" and should listen to competent pediatricians instead of Jenny McCarthy, referring to the actor who blames her son's autism on the MMR vaccine, and vigorously promotes her anti-MMR cause.

Pro-vaxers occasionally resorted to sarcasm that was just mild enough to avoid bullying but strong enough to avoid misinterpretation. Given Dell'Antonia's headline, "Should Unvaccinated Children Stay Home to Protect a Vulnerable Classmate?" Ian (January 30, 2015) responded, "No. They should go to school and endanger the classmate's life." Ian added, "The NYTimes—always on the cutting edge." Responding to anti-vaxers who knew people who survived measles, Banty AcidJazz (January 22, 2015) drew fifty-two recommendations when he noted that as children, he and his siblings survived both measles and not using seatbelts. "Let's get rid of seat belt laws," he joked. A variety of analogies and/or connections to other extreme movements were offered, from home schooling to anti-fluoridation activism.

That said, katieatl (January 22, 2015) was one of many to criticize a pro-vaxer's "mean" tone: "People should stick to the facts and leave out their opinions about others' 'primitive' religions and need for a 'stupid exception.' Condescension is rarely persuasive." Pediatrician X (February 4, 2015) criticized a specific poster's "snark." Allen (January 22, 2015) went to pains to remind *Motherlode* posters that anti-vaxers are not bad parents, just dangerously misinformed. Mary (February 4, 2015) urged "compassion and acknowledgement for families living through this. ... Please honor the little fallen soldiers in this war on disease instead of shaming and belittling their parents that dare to speak up ...." Exemplifying the strong language used to condemn anti-vaxers as a group, SpittingKitty (February 4, 2015) wrote: "What about the rights of those of us who don't believe a bunch of tin-foil-hat-wearing malarkey? We should be able to send our kids to school without worrying about little Typhoid

Mary and her conspiracy theorist parent." Yet, pro-vaxers tactfully expressed sympathy and concern for individuals whose children allegedly suffered illnesses. Developing a theme raised by Peachman, dozens of posters speculated that anti-vaxers didn't understand the dangers of certain diseases because they never saw them; it was apparently because of this that many people mentioned relatives who suffered from polio, or were deaf or blind because of measles. Perhaps the explanation for commenters' civilized tone, which rose to the level of snark but never attack when responding to individuals on both vaccinations and free-range parenting, is that this aligned with the *Motherlode* community's sense of itself as educated, thoughtful, and political, as well as the policy of comment moderation.

The moral status of freedom

The dominant theme was freedom. Pro-vaxers posted a tension between individual freedom and collective or civic good. As Tim McEown (February 4, 2015) put it: "Society operates in a tension between individual rights and communal obligations." Anti-vaxers posited a tension between individual freedom and governmental action. Others said they had vaccinated their children but worried that government mandates impinged on individual freedoms. Insisting he was no anti-vaxer, WhackyDad (February 3, 2015) said he feared a government with absolute control over what goes into his body, adding: "A government that has the power to force vaccinations on its citizens to control disease also has the power to force abortions on women to prevent overpopulation." Melissa (February 4, 2015) likewise worried about parents' "personal freedoms to choose what medical products are being injected into their children's bodies." Melissa's reference to measles as a generally non-life threatening disease was immediately repudiated, although people refused to engage with her sarcastic prediction of "quarantine (concentration camps maybe??)" for non-vaccinated children. Calling forced vaccination "uncomfortably close to legal assault," Bookworm8571 (February 3, 2015) noted many other laws could be passed that would also make things safer but would cause erosion of civil liberties: "How much of your personal freedom and individual rights are you willing to give up for increased safety?" However, many responders noted that vaccinations were not forced, but were voluntary for home-schooled children.

Many more vehemently and repeatedly repudiated the logic of freedom, such as Anon (a trusted commenter; February 4, 2015) who provided a long list of (frequently invisible) restraints that "civil, safe society depends on" and showing that "your government has the authority to impinge in countless ways on 'individual preference and choice.'" Rosie (NYC, February 4, 2015) agreed that "your rights end when mine start": "Yours and your family's rights end when your actions are going to hurt somebody else's family's and personal rights." Even more, the risks to children who could not themselves be vaccinated brought a vehement repudiation of neoliberal individualism and its emphasis on individual freedom. EK (February 3, 2015) agreed: "Rights come with responsibilities. Parents that don't vaccinate their kids are not upholding their end of the social contract."

The status of science

All three articles evoked technical or medical explanations. Among others, people who said they were nurses or doctors included urls to medical research. Anti-vaxers posted links to the popular press and to anti-vaccination "experts." Technical answers were offered to a variety of claims—but also explicit questions. Peachman, for example, raised concerns about her daughter who was not yet old enough for her second MMR dose: "What if her little body has not yet mounted an adequate immune response to her first MMR dose?" Several people immediately replied.

But while the pro-vaxers seemed proud of their scientific knowledge, they rejected the neoliberal notion that parents must not trust medical professionals. Therefore, the main question for pro-vaxers was whether they should bother arguing with anti-vaxers who thought they knew better than doctors. Di (January 22, 2015) cited studies showing that "the more you argue with these people, the more right they think they are." Many agreed that anti-vaxers are immune to rational arguments. Rosie (February 4, 2015) asserted

> You can't reason with people driven by fear, ignorance and paranoia. No matter the evidence, those people will believe what they want to believe but the rest of us do not have to put up with their non-sense. Let's stop wasting time trying to show them the evidence and just start protecting those of us who know better even if we have to offend some misguided sensibilities.

Separately that day, Rosie invoked Stephen Colbert when she predicted problems if society allows "'truthiness' and religion to trump reason and evidence in the public space." On the other hand, Bismarck (February 3, 2015) asserted "an obligation to engage the anti-vaccinators, loudly and frequently."

Motherlode *and free-range parenting*

Danielle and Alexander Meitiv had prepared their children for walking independently over time, first letting them go around the block, then to a 7-Eleven a little farther away, to a library, and finally the mile to and from the park. Alexander regarded the police intervention as a nanny-state intrusion, recalling his childhood in the former Soviet Union, where public officials pried often and with impunity into citizens' private lives (Hanna Rosin 2015). CPS investigated the Meitivs for child neglect. Five months later the children were again walking alone. Police picked them up and held them for more than five hours, which led to a second neglect investigation of the parents. Child Protective Services authorities cleared the Meitivs the following month, in June 2015.

At one end of the parenting spectrum are free-range parents, who believe that children must learn to be independent and self-reliant from an early age by being given greater freedoms, learning to make choices, and being less supervised. At the other end are "helicopter" parents, who foreground parental responsibility and risk in every encounter, representing the intensive model at its most extreme. For Lenore Skenazy, parenting today has become hyper-focused on over-protecting children from the dangers supposedly lurking around every corner and even the expected bumps in the road: "In just one generation, what was considered a normal, happy, HEALTHY childhood has become considered WILDLY dangerous. Litigiously dangerous" (http://www.freerangekids.com/faq/#4).

Dell'Antonia (2015a) quoted *Washington Post* columnist Petula Dvorak's critique of intensive parenting: when parents are not allowed to encourage independence, "not only are we placing unreasonable demands on parents to be with their children 24/7, but we are stunting the natural development that creates independent humans." Describing her own parenting practices as in line with those of free-rangers, Dell'Antonia noted that her eleven-year-old got his first grade and third grade siblings off the school bus, bought them a snack at a store and walked everyone to an after-school art class.

The free-range parenting posters regularly debated whether millennial parenting culture is worse for kids than the looser, freer environment that they had enjoyed as youths. FearlessLdr (April 13, 2015) remembered a free-range childhood in New Jersey, riding bicycles to the beach and swimming all day. "No parents to be seen." Commenters lamented the loss of freedom and the independence kids enjoyed in the past, and worried about the effects of that loss. Leo Van Groll (April 19, 2015) recalled being ten and riding his bike to a state park fifteen miles away, adding: "Today's sheltered children are growing up to be tomorrow's socially awkward loners with their noses buried in their smartphones." Meanwhile, many people argued that the world is actually safer now than in decades past, although social media and news cycles feature 24/7 news of AMBER alerts and other situations involving harm to children.

Others fiercely contested this memory of an idealized childhood as a dangerous myth. ACO (January 19, 2015) rejected a glorious free-range past:

> I get so tired of hearing all the romanticized tales of the 70s. Yes we had those magical long days outside wandering the neighborhood, but they were punctuated by some very serious, very troubling moments that happened out of the eyes and ears of any parents.

Steve (July 5, 2015) reminded readers of the many children pictured on milk cartons who disappeared while walking home alone: "Perhaps now we could hear from some of the many children who were assaulted, harassed, bullied, and yes, kidnapped, raped and beaten?"

The operative term for posters responding to the Meitiv case was *risk*. Dell'Antonia helped to set the terms of the debate by foregrounding risk in her second post, "As Parents Stand on Principle, Are 'Free-Range' Children Put at Risk?" The photograph that accompanied her post was captioned: "When is a walk a risk?" No matter which side of the free-range question posters came down on, many commenters view modern parenting as a complex exercise in risk management. In the absence of consensus (and indeed, this inevitably varies by city and neighborhood) about when children can safely begin to learn to handle independence or which places are safe, the Meitivs' decision to allow their children to walk alone was controversial. Parent Lyn Morgan (April 14, 2015) described her approach precisely in those terms: "It's more about making decisions about the risks vs benefits about a situation, then ensuring precautions are taken to minimize the risks so the benefits can be enjoyed." The benefit, of course, is the cultivation of a "successful" child whose significant academic and extracurricular achievements bode well for a competitive future. Nate Awrich (April 13, 2015) noted: "Life is filled with risks, balancing them for other people's children is not your job or your right." That is, a neoliberal parent must balance risk for *one's own children*.

Motherlode commenters identified and debated numerous kinds of risk associated with free-range parenting, beginning with the risk of inviting state intervention and surveillance. VV (January 16, 2015) insisted that this threat outweighed the benefit of giving children more freedom.

> The ability of Child Services to intervene in our life … scares me more than the risk to my kids. I am able to judge the latter, knowing my kids maturity and readiness, but I don't feel prepared to deal and defend us effectively to Child Services or police.

Jen (January 16, 2015) concurred, noting that she would not allow her daughter to walk alone for fear of being reported: "The danger from the authorities is greater than the risk to her person." Zeke (April 21, 2015) wrote that parents should do whatever was necessary to avoid CPS investigation, even if it meant parenting in ways that did not feel authentic. "If your belief system, whether it is your religion or parenting philosophy means it puts your family at risk of being torn from you—perhaps it's time to change your beliefs. I would."

Posters similarly debated whether citizens ought to inform on parents. Several insisted that calling CPS was justified whenever inadequate parenting was suspected. In agreeing, Jeanne (January 16, 2005) catalogued the threats to unsupervised children: "pedophiles (and worse), bullies, animal attacks (domestic and wild), falling and injuries, sudden weather conditions, emergencies, etc." But, many contested this position. "Please deliver us from nosey neighbors with cell phones and 911 speed dial buttons," wrote Oliver Clarke (April 14, 2015). E.G. (April 13, 2015) criticized the "terrible thing that neighbor did by calling 911 on the parents."

Many comments revolved around the larger threat of state intervention in family life. Bill Randle (January 16, 2015) found it "very, very disturbing that the state thinks they have the right to come into someone's home and make demands merely because the children have been taught how to get around their neighborhood safely." KJ Dell'Antonia ratcheted up repeated laments that Child and Family Services "have more power than the police" when she confessed in a follow-up (2015e) that if her parenting attracted CPS attention, she would "stand down rather than risk martyring my children in the name of principle." Directly responding, Bill Michtom (April 14, 2015) called Dell'Antonia's willingness to obey the state "appalling." But Me (April 14, 2015) doubted that she would have the courage to stand up for her parenting principles against CPS demands. Fear would lead her to "give into government sanctioned parenting." For many, including Dell'Antonia, the answer apparently was that erring on the side of "giving in" was the better course of action.

Indeed, some commenters worried that the threat alone affected parents' behavior. dobes (April 14, 2015) warned about the consequences of tailoring parenting to meet neoliberal state expectations: "If the threat of having our kids removed makes us all stand down … then they can be sure we will all comply, every time, with even the most intrusive, egregious rules." Bookworm 8,571 (April 14, 2015) likewise worried: "When parents knuckle under, a precedent is set and everyone else loses some of their freedoms." cbg (April 15, 2015) saw this extending to other arenas where the state might dictate decisions that may rightfully belong to parents: "If my pediatrician recommends Ritalin for my child I am afraid to say no because I may be labeled a negligent or noncompliant parent …." AB (April 13, 2015) said she would personally never leave her child in a car, even for a moment, "because I would be afraid of a public shaming, not because I really believed it was wrong."

Parenting in ways that meet public expectations and avoid trauma to children, albeit that feel inauthentic, seemed to be a common experience. Dell'Antonia wrote that she would accommodate state demands rather than risk trauma to her children. Yet, commenters characterized both free-range and intensive parents as threats to their children. Many described the Meitivs as selfish, and as too stubborn or ideologically rigid. M Bernard (April 14, 2015) argued:

> Instead of traumatizing their children over their need to make a political statement, these folks should just follow the laws like the rest of us and allow their children to have a childhood without knowing what it feels like to sit in the back of a police car.

Yet, some commenters claimed that parents who risk-manage too assiduously create a different type of threat to their children. AM (April 14, 2015), who claimed to use free-range methods, wrote that the surest way for parents to put their children at risk "is to limit their children's development, experience, judgment, and knowledge of the world, based on exaggerated fear, simple-mindedness, and misinformation." Several emphasized the importance of children learning to function independently. Vehemently responding to one intensive parent prioritizing safety, Cal Bears 1 (January 16, 2015) disagreed: "A thousand times NO! The No. 1 job for parents is to give children the resources (emotional, educational, physical) to become happy, curious, independent people."

Conclusion: parents' critique of news media

Prominent in the commentary is a savvy understanding of media political economy. Blog participants criticized how media framed issues and consistently recognized skirmishes as a cynical attempt to attract audiences. They connected media-driven fears about safety and the "24/7 fear mongering 'news' networks that must fill the time somehow, scaring people" (Anne, April 13, 2015) with intensive parenting and a neoliberal agenda to privatize childcare responsibilities, noting that one aided and abetted the other. Quinn (April 13, 2015) urged readers to consider why the world seemed so much "scarier" than in the past: "Perhaps part of the reason is that the news media has reinforced our fears with an endless cycle of programming that hypes every event." L (January 16, 2015) blamed "today's world of information over-saturation and 24-h news cycle sensationalism" for creating fear among parents, leading to the kind of "overreach in response" that led to the Meitiv investigations.

But participants' vigorous and widely shared rejection of media hype did not prevent commenters—both women and men—from thoughtful self-reflexive consideration of parenting practices and expectations, especially the pressure they feel to accommodate to the intensive parenting model. Audience members' everyday discursive activity on *Motherlode* shows why such blogs are important to parents struggling to figure out how they can best rear their children. Blogs provide a space to do more than simply encounter major parenting issues and to get daily support. They are also an outlet in which to critique, explain, and analyze the entire modern project of parenting and how it is pushed down to individuals by the state and sold by the media. They clearly stage the workings of contemporary parenting ideology—and the guilt about the potential consequences of ignoring neoliberal mandates.[9] Almost never seeming to notice that the *New York Times* was sponsoring their critiques, they picked up on what journalists rarely admit, that, despite the paucity of evidence for Mommy Wars, "Everybody loves a catfight, none more so than the news media" (Caryl Rivers 2007, 62). V (January 16, 2015) argued that in the era when most mothers stayed at home, giving children some independence was acceptable. Only when many mothers began working outside the home were the same attitudes and behaviors redefined as risky. V offered a sophisticated understanding of the connections among neoliberalism, anti-feminism, intensive parenting, and the twenty-four-hour news cycle:

> The push for "safety" is actually a way to nicely package cultural backlash against the liberation of women and their entry into the workforce. It's about trying to push moms back into the home. And kids, moms and dads are suffering and suffocating because of it.

Again, this is fiercely debated. Most commenters on the two issues understood *Motherlode* as a political space where they could challenge gendered-skewed conceptions that blame mothers for children's failures or shortcomings. But Anon (April 16, 2015) warned: "[W]hen you leave your young children unattended you are relinquishing control over what happens to them to other adults they may encounter." That is, parents who ignore intensive norms are responsible for whatever harms may befall their children.

Because the site is heavily moderated, determining what or who may have been kept out is impossible, although the blog editors claim to be guided by civility, not politics. Dell'Antonia responded several times to technical or medical questions, quietly offering additional facts or promising to undertake further investigation, and occasionally quoting posters in her columns or follow-ups. When commentators once asked for details confirming one mother's account, Dell'Antonia (February 4, 2015) stepped in to assert that the commenter was willing to provide this information, but that *Motherlode* was not the place to do it. She had therefore ended the thread out of privacy concerns. In any case, for all issues and sides, citizen "sheep" were an anathema, as indicated by free-range advocate Craig Millett's (April 15, 2015) observation that "whiny paranoia for the dears will make wonderful sheep but not so much able humans who have any self-confidence out in the real world." But when anti-vaxer SamK (February 4, 2015) decried "sheep willing to allow themselves to be jabbed by an unknown substance," Jennifer S (February 4, 2015) confidently asserted "that almost everyone here is educated and has thought this through …. Please stop referring to everyone who doesn't buy into every conspiracy theory thrown at their doorstep as sheep."

The importance of a space like *Motherlode*, whose seriousness is masked by the use of a juvenile label like mommyblog, comes from allowing average audience members—neither celebrities nor other public figures—to provide detailed explanations and critiques of the quotidian pressures they face as parents. When citizenship is redefined as an exercise in consumer choice, rather than an orientation to the collective good, vaccination is reframed as a personal health decision, just as free-range parenting invites punitive state intervention instead of affirmations of communal responsibility for child welfare. Either way, the discussions that take place on such blogs help parents negotiate the everyday politics of raising children. These blogs allow parents to support or question and contest the norms of intensive parenting and neoliberal individualism, thus allowing audience members to face head on their anxieties about modern parenthood, especially the risk–reward calculations that otherwise can be so agonizing.

Notes

1. During the California gold rush, miners followed the gold-bearing sands upstream to discover the source of the gold, the so-called "mother lode."
2. A particular blog may, of course, attract a particular taste public; and parenting sites can take different approaches, including ones inflected by race, ethnicity, sexual orientation, and economic or political privilege. *Motherlode* editor KJ Dell'Antonia (2015d) has lightly bragged about her "A list" commenters but does not indicate how her philosophy or the site tilts toward a specific kind of educated middle-class audience.
3. Scholars and bloggers increasingly regard the term mommyblogs as trivializing, but the alternative "mom blog" has not been embraced.
4. That is, the *New York Times* is for-profit, but the specific site offers a forum for discussion and information exchange that is not product based.
5. Capitalizing on the marketing opportunity that arose when journalists dubbed her "America's Worst Mom," Skenazy promotes her response to "fear soup" (fear of lawsuits, injury, abductions, blame) in speeches, a website, and a book (Lenore Skenazy 2009) debunking a variety of parental fears and media-sponsored hysteria.
6. *Motherlode* ran articles dealing with all sorts of vaccinations, such as HPV and flu.
7. Each author drafted one issue, but read all posts and comments regarding the other issue; and we consulted regarding interpretation.

8. Dell'Antonia (2015d) says she rejects comments that are inflammatory, name-calling, rude, irrelevant, incoherent, or obscene. In any case, the vast majority of responses to her explanation expressed deep appreciation of her "moderation." WhackyDad, however, objected: "To think we need mommy to filter out any post that might be offensive is an insult to those of us who participate. So what if we get an occasional troll? ... [I]f I get called a jerk or some other unflattering name every now and then, I can handle it."
9. We thank the editors of this special issue for this point.

Disclosure statement

No potential conflict of interest was reported by the authors.

References

Akass, Kim. 2012. "Motherhood and Myth-Making: Despatches from the Frontline of the US Mommy Wars." *Feminist Media Studies* 12 (1): 137–141.

Belkin, Lisa. 2003. "The Opt-Out Revolution". *New York Times Magazine*, October 26: 42–47, 58, 85–86.

Blair-Loy, Mary. 2003. *Competing Devotions: Career and Family among Women Executives*. Cambridge: Harvard University Press.

Blum, Linda. 2007. "Mother-Blame in the Prozac Nation: Raising Kids with Invisible Disabilities." *Gender & Society* 21 (2): 202–226.

Braedley, Susan, and Meg Luxton. 2010. *Neoliberalism and Everyday Life*. Toronto: McGill-Queen's Press.

Christopher, Karen. 2012. "Extensive Mothering: Employed Mothers' Constructions of the Good Mother." *Gender & Society* 26 (1): 73–96.

Collins, Patricia. 1994. "Shifting the Center: Race, Class, and Feminist Theorizing about Motherhood." In *Mothering: Ideology, Experience, and Agency*, edited by Evelyn N. Glenn, Grace Chang, and Linda R. Forcey, 45–66. New York: Routledge.

Dell'Antonia, KJ. 2015a. "When Did 'Teaching Independence' Become 'Possible Neglect'?" *Motherlode*, January 15. http://parenting.blogs.nytimes.com/2015/01/15/when-did-teaching-independence-become-possible-neglect/?_r=0

Dell'Antonia, KJ. 2015b. "Should Unvaccinated Children Stay Home to Protect a Vulnerable Classmate?" *Motherlode*, January 29. http://parenting.blogs.nytimes.com/2015/01/29/should-unvaccinated-children-to-stay-home-to-protect-a-vulnerable-classmate/

Dell'Antonia, KJ. 2015c. "Want More Vaccinated Kids? End Religious and Personal Exemptions." *Motherlode*, February 2. http://parenting.blogs.nytimes.com/2015/02/02/want-more-vaccinated-children-end-religious-and-personal-exemptions/

Dell'Antonia, KJ. 2015d. "Motherlode's 'Celebrity Class of Commenters.'" *Motherlode*, February 26. http://parenting.blogs.nytimes.com/2015/02/26/motherlodes-celebrity-class-of-commenters/?_r=0

Dell'Antonia, KJ. 2015e. "As Parents Stand on Principle, Are 'Free-Range' Children Put at Risk?" *Motherlode*, April 13. http://parenting.blogs.nytimes.com/2015/04/13/as-parents-stand-on-principle-are-free-range-children-put-at-risk/

Caputo, Virginia. 2007. "She's from a 'Good Family': Performing Childhood and Motherhood in a Canadian Private School Setting." *Childhood* 14 (2): 173–192.

Douglas, Susan, and Meredith Michaels. 2004. *The Mommy Myth: The Idealization of Motherhood and How It Has Undermined All Women*. New York: Free Press.

Ericson, Richard V., Aaron Doyle, and Dean Barry. 2003. *Insurance as Governance*. Toronto: University of Toronto Press.

Fraser, Nancy. 2013. *Fortunes of Feminism: From State-Managed Capitalism to Neoliberal Crisis*. London: Verso.

Furedi, Frank. 2008. *Paranoid Parenting*. London: Continuum.

Gilbert, Jeremy. 2013. "What Kind of Thing is Neoliberalism." *New Formations* 80/81: 7–22.

Graff, E. J. 2007. "The Mommy War Machine." *The Washington Post*, April 29. http://www.washingtonpost.com/wpdyn/content/article/2007/04/27/AR2007042702043.html

Gulbransen, Scott. 2012. "Mommy Blogging by the Numbers." May 8. http://blogs.hrblock.com/2012/05/08/mommy-blogging-by-the-numbers-infographic/

Gust, Deborah A., Natalie Darling, Allison Kennedy, and Ben Schwartz. 2008. "Parents with Doubts about Vaccines: Which Vaccines and Reasons Why." *Pediatrics* 122 (4): 718–725.

Hall, Stuart. 1975. "Introduction." In *Paper Voices: The Popular Press and Social Change 1935-1965*, edited by Anthony Charles H. Smith, with Elizabeth Immirzi, and Trevor Blackwell, 11-24. London: Chatto and Windus.

Hays, Sharon. 1996. *The Cultural Contradictions of Motherhood*. New Haven, CT: Yale University Press.

Hobson-West, Pru. 2007. "'Trusting Blindly Can Be the Biggest Risk of All': Organised Resistance to Childhood Vaccination in the UK." *Sociology of Health & Illness* 29 (2): 198–215.

Hoffman, Diane M. 2010. "Risky Investments: Parenting and the Production of the 'Resilient Child.'" *Health, Risk & Society* 12 (4): 385-394.

Johnston, Deirdre D., and Debra H. Swanson. 2007. "Cognitive Acrobatics in the Construction of Worker–Mother Identity." *Sex Roles* 57 (5-6): 447–459.

Kido-Lopez, Lori. 2009. "The Radical Act of 'Mommy Blogging': Redefining Motherhood through the Blogosphere." *New Media & Society* 11 (5): 729–747.

Knaak, Stephanie J. 2010. "Contextualizing Risk, Constructing Choice: Breastfeeding and Good Mothering in Risk Society." *Health, Risk & Society* 12 (4): 345–355.

Lee, Ellie, Jan Macvarish, and Jennie Bristow. 2010. "Risk, Health, and Parenting Culture." *Health, Risk & Society* 12 (4): 293–300.

Marse, Amie. 2013. "A Surprising B2B Content Target Demographic: Moms.", April 8. http://b2binsights.com/a-surprising-b2b-content-target-demographic-moms/

McDaniel, Brandon, Sarah Coyne, and Erin Holmes. 2012. "New Mothers and Media Use: Associations between Blogging, Social Networking, and Maternal Well-Being." *Maternal and Child Health Journal* 16: 1509–1517.

McRobbie, Angela. 2013. "Feminism, the Family and the New 'Mediated' Maternalism." *New Formations* 80: 119–137.

Morrison, Aimée. 2011. "'Suffused by Feeling and Affect': The Intimate Public of Personal Mommy Blogging." *Biography* 34 (1): 37–55.

Orgad, Shani, and Sara De Benedictis. 2015. "The 'Stay-at-Home' Mother, Postfeminism and Neoliberalism: Content Analysis of UK News Coverage." *European Journal of Communication* 30 (4): 418–436.

Peachman, Rachel Rabkin. 2015. "When Measles Spreads from Disneyland, It's a Small World after All." *Motherlode*, January 21. http://parenting.blogs.nytimes.com/2015/01/21/when-measles-spreads-from-disneyland-its-a-small-world-after-all/

Poltorak, Mike, Melissa Leach, James Fairhead, and Jackie Cassell. 2005. "MMR Talk and Vaccination Choices: An Ethnographic Study in Brighton." *Social Science and Medicine* 61 (3): 709–719.

Reich, Jennifer A. 2014. "Neoliberal Mothering and Vaccine Refusal: Imagined Gated Communities and the Privilege of Choice." *Gender & Society* 28 (5): 679–704.

Rivers, Caryl. 2007. *Selling Anxiety: How the News Media Scare Women*. Lebanon, NH: UPNE.

Rosenthal, Andrew. 2012. "Is There a Chief Comments Moderator?" *New York times*, March 13. http://takingnote.blogs.nytimes.com/2012/03/13/is-there-a-chief-comments-moderator/?_r=0

Rosin, Hanna. 2015. "Police Investigate Family for Letting Their Kids Walk Home Alone, Parents: We All Need to Fight Back."*Slate*, January 16. Accessed January 1, 2016. http://www.slate.com/blogs/xx_factor/2015/01/16/maryland_parents_investigated_by_the_police_for_letting_their_kids_walk.html

Sender, Katherine. 2015. "Reconsidering Reflexivity: Audience Research and Reality Television." *The Communication Review* 18 (1): 37–52.

Shaw, Frances. 2013. "'These Wars Are Personal': Methods and Theory in Online Feminist Research." *Qualitative Research Journal* 13 (1): 90-101.

Skenazy, Lenore. 2008. "Why I Let My 9-Year-Old Ride the Subway Alone." *The New York Sun*, April 1. http://www.nysun.com/opinion/why-i-let-my-9-year-old-ride-subway-alone/73976/

Skenazy, Lenore. 2009. *Free-Range Kids: Giving Our Children the Freedom We Had without Going Nuts with Worry*. San Francisco: Jossey-Bass.

Wall, Glenda. 2001. "Moral Constructions of Motherhood in Breastfeeding Discourse." *Gender & Society* 15 (4): 592–610.

Zimmerman, Toni Schindler, Jennifer T. Aberle, Jennifer L. Krafchick, and Ashley M. Harvey. 2008. "Deconstructing the 'Mommy Wars': The Battle over the Best Mom." *Journal of Feminist Family Therapy* 20 (3): 203–219.

MirrorCameraRoom: the gendered multi-(in)stabilities of the selfie

Katie Warfield

ABSTRACT

This paper proposes benefits of the entanglement of feminist new materialist theory with post-phenomenology. The paper focuses on an empirical study of interviews using photo-elicitation with four young women to document their lived experiences producing self-images to share via social media. Drawing on post-phenomenology, the cellphone is discussed as a multi-stable technology wherein the selfie is experienced at once as a *mirror*, a *camera*, and a *window* to social media platforms. But this paper also draws on *glitch* feminism, which, via metaphors of technological failure, challenges ossified conceptual boundaries between the body, desire, and technology. Through this coupling the paper suggests that what are identified as corporeal, photographic, and performative *glitches* by the participants are worked out, thereby erasing any experiential delineation between mirror, camera, and cellphone. Whereas post-phenomenology often refrains from examining the complex power dynamics that shape technological–human relations, this paper argues that such dynamics are crucial when examining gendered technological phenomena like selfies. Contributing empirical data to recent post-phenomenological work on cellphones, this paper details the gendered material-discursive dimensions of the selfie via the work of contemporary feminist new materialist thinkers.

Introduction

In 2009, Sonia Livingstone and Ranjana Das famously questioned the "end of audiences." Mark Deuze (2012) suggests that in our increasingly mediated lives, perhaps *we are the medium*. Theorists of Internet and social media studies have tackled similar befuddling questions where we've become at once producers and consumers—*pro-sumers* (Alvin Toffler 1980)—or simultaneously producers and users—*produsers* (Karl Fahringer and Axel Bruns 2008). Studying audiences at this period in history is like "wrestling with a jellyfish" (Justin Lewis 2013) because, among other things, audiences could be both *always and everywhere* (Peter Vorderer and Matthias Kohring 2013) or *everywhere and nowhere* (Elizabeth Bird 2003).

The selfie—a "photo one has taken of oneself typically one taken with a smartphone or webcam and shared via social media" (Oxford English Dictionary 2015)—and what I'll address in this paper, is in many ways a social media jellyfish that epitomizes the contemporary gauze-like status of the classic borderlines separating producers, texts, and audiences. When I produce a selfie, I am taking an image of myself and so I become both the *producer* and the *text*. In the process of selecting which image to share, I wonder: to what *imagined audience* (Bernie Hogan 2010) will this self-image be distributed: my welcoming audience of Tumblr™ or my more discriminating audience of Facebook™? I share a given image with an audience often not only based on expected performance (Erving Goffman 1974) but on my networked *affective* relations with those people (Ken Hillis, Susanna Paasonen, and Michael Petit 2015). As *producers* become *texts*, and as *audiences* are folded under our skin, our traditional approaches are challenged: how are we to analyze and learn from such a multidimensional material and discursive phenomenon[1] like the selfie?

Given this complexity, the frameworks of analysis used for study of the selfie have been equally diverse but tend to generally fall in one of three categories: selfies are presentation, representation, and embodiment (Amparo Lasén and Edgar Gómez-Cruz 2009). As *presentation*, selfies could be considered along the traditions of Goffman (1974) and Judith Butler (1988): a performance to an audience or a play of an anticipated role. As *representation*, selfies could be textual and communicative, and deconstructed and read semiotically (Jill Walker Rettberg 2014). As *embodiment*, selfies can transmit affective qualities and evoke the materiality of the body (Jessica Ringrose and Emma Renold 2014; Theresa M. Senft 2015). The seeming exclusivity in the application of each of these categories is intriguing: can selfies not do or be *more than one* of these things simultaneously?

In this paper I respond to audience research and this query with not just an eye, but also with a turn of my fully-mediated body, to what I'd like to propose is the increasingly gauze-like status of the screen—especially for young women who are often rebuked as the major producers of selfies. This paper asks: what does a group of young women experience in the process of producing a selfie? I examine this question via interviews and photo elicitation with four young women from Vancouver, Canada who are self-described avid selfie takers.

I tangle together post-phenomenology with the feminist new materialist-influenced theories of glitch feminism (Legacy Russell 2012). Post-phenomenology, which combines pragmatism with phenomenology, permits us to view the changing, dynamic, malleable, and plastic nature of our experiences with technology. As such the cellphone is discussed as a post-phenomenological *multi-stable* technology (Don Ihde 2012; Galit P. Wellner 2016), which means that, for this group of young women, the cellphone is experienced as multiple consolidated technologies in one device: a mirror, a camera, and a door to a social media platform. Injecting a more critical approach, I then present how these material technologies have historically been constructed as discursively gendered.

While understanding the selfie as a post-phenomenological phenomenon, I am further interested in investigating those particular moments that arise in the process of selfie taking: *glitches*. Whereas stability brackets a user from their experience of a cellphone in one moment as a camera, and at the next moment a social media platform, a glitch is an interruption of these clearly bounded spaces. Following Russell (2012) and the growing literature on glitch feminism, I want to propose that it is the glitches that *puncture* the screen and destabilize the presumed to be stable and separate phenomenological stabilities within the encounter with the cellphone (Roland Barthes and Richard Howard 1982). A glitch offers a crack, an opening. A glitch turns what is presumed to be solid into that which is fluid. Glitch feminism, then, looks for these openings and examines how glitches work to cross boundaries, connect divisions, and destabilize presumptions of stability and stasis. I examine the different glitches that arise when the cellphone is used in its different invariants: corporeal glitches appear with the cellphone-as-mirror, representational glitches appear with the cellphone-as-camera, and presentational or performative glitches appear with the cellphone-as-social-media-door. Taking different forms, glitches connect one stability or *invariant* to another—the experience of the mirror entangling more intimately with the experience of the camera entangling more closely with the experience of the door to social media. I propose that the glitches crack the mirror, puncture the photo, and slightly unhinge the door. In the discussion section I suggest that glitches turn the screen from a conceptually hard surface to what it is experientially described by this group of young women as similar to a gauze-like, permeable, and intimate *plank* (Russell 2012) bridging the self, the world, and technology (*I–world–technology*) (Ihde 2012).

Post-phenomenology and glitch feminism

Following recent post-phenomenological research, particularly the work of Wellner (2016), the cellphone in this paper is considered a *multi-stable* technology. Ihde (2012) suggests that contemporary digital technologies, unlike older technologies, are increasingly *multi-stable*. Whereas a technology like a hammer seems to afford limited options for use—striking is the dominant affordance—technologies like screens on computers can serve many overlapping purposes: they can display the flat text of a journal article and be read like a book one minute, and then in a Gestalt shift, the screen can display the experientially 3D interactive world of an online game. In a third moment, the cellphone may shift to connect, via video conference, the image of a real-time colleague halfway around the world. Ihde (2012) uses the phenomenological experiences of the Gestalt shift to describe I–technology–world *shifts* that occur when we toggle phenomenologically between the different temporarily stable, but *multiple*, stabilities of the *multi*-stable cellphone.

New technologies don't cancel out old ones, they "sublate"—meaning they continually compound *on top of* old ones instead of erasing them (Wellner 2016). This makes sense when we think of the multitude of functions our cellphones can occasion: phone, video recorder, notepad, videogame console, social media interface, and the list goes on. How this multiplicity affects, over time, the experience with a multi-stable technology is called an *invariant*. Invariants are *structuring patterns or common denominators* in an historical variation (Wellner 2016). In her discussion of the cellphone, Wellner (2016) illustrates how the design and affordances of a cellphone may vary (historical variation) but the invariant of the *wall–window* remains the same, where no matter the cellphone variation, it commonly acts as a *wall* separating the person with the device from their immediate surroundings, and a *window* to different connected experiences online.

Wellner (2016) clearly states that a focal point of her research program is not the material or discursive structures of power that have historically shaped technologies. But this paper challenges the bracketing of the political to the realm of discourse, and the material to the everyday. In this next section, via feminist new materialist thinking, I discuss empirical data that suggest any study of the *histories of the future*, as post-phenomenology aims to do, *cannot* neglect power dynamics as they increasingly manifest both materially and discursively via technological encounters and through our embodied experiences.

Feminist new materialism and glitch feminism

The proposition I'm making here, about the importance of material and discursive entanglements of power, aligns with a common theme in feminist new materialism: the rejection of *a priori* delineations between discursively ossified categories like the mind as separate and distinct from the body, the discursive as separate from the material, and the human as separate from non-human (Karen Barad 2007; Rosi Braidotti 2001; Rick Dolphijn and Iris van der Tuin 2012). By *post-representational*, what new materialism does is suggest that the conceptual metaphor of the *representation* has benefits as well as pitfalls. Representationalism is the crux of the discursive turn where words are seen as entities that then interact with and upon material things like bodies: images affect bodies, words affect actions. A post-representational approach argues that entities *do not* preexist their surroundings—at an ontological level, we aren't looking at entities within a void—words within nothing—but rather potentials entangled within fields. As an example Karen Barad discusses concepts like the body and subjectivity not as *a priori* and bounded *things*, but as potentialities whose boundaries are defined again and anew within the specific entanglements of their surroundings in a given moment through time. This is why Barad uses the term *intra-action* instead of *inter-action* (Barad 2007). Inter-action presumes the preexistence of bounded objects that then interact. Intra-action begins with entanglement—the connection of everything. I'm interested in the intra-action or becoming of the selfie via the complex entanglement of bodies, sense of self, gender, and affect, alongside technologies and imaging processes, through history.

In this post-humanist vein, and inspired by the online sexual encounters of her youth, Russell (2012) coined the term *glitch feminism* to refer to the irruption of desire that happens online and between body–technology encounters. Russell developed glitch feminism in reaction to Nathan Jurgensen's (2011) naming of the concept *digital dualism* which proposed there is an online self that is fundamentally separate and distinct from an offline self. Russell (2012) challenges digital dualism arguing that the phenomenon of the technological *glitch*—the spinning wheel of the O/S, the flicker of malformed pixels—evoked not a separation of online from offline but instead hooked the corporeal body more completely to its interactions with the technology. In the moment of glitch, the computer demands a pause and the background-ness of the technology (Martin Heidegger and William Lovitt 1978) via the glitch, becomes the *technology-in-hand*—clearly visible to the user (Jason Farman 2014). The glitch marks a reminder of the give-and-take that always exists in *any* body–technology encounter. Further, Russell (2012) describes this give-and-take as experienced by the user as a form of sensual technological *foreplay*. As such it is affective and a reminder of our phenomenologically intimate relationship with technology, wherein a sensual online connection with another person, for instance, is also an intimate *three-way* with technology.

A glitch, as Russell (2012) puts it, orgasmically produces a "sigh, a shudder, and a jerk spasm" (3) that creates a *plank* passing between the offline and online. Jenny Sundén (2015) highlights other post-human qualities of the glitch: "glitch is a struggle with binaries" (9) since the technological glitch is often the result of a lost, or a misreading of, binary code. Technologically the glitch is fundamentally a rejection or failure of binaries. Sundén (2015) suggests that the glitch may be seen as a correction to the norms or the programming of the *machine*, and in turn a positive departure for both technology and the study of gender, whose projects historically have been founded on outwardly rigid but profoundly slippery and fragile binaries.

The study: photo elicitation with post-phenomenological analysis

I began the data collection with an interest in what young women actually experience when they take selfies? What are their thoughts and feelings while facing the camera, editing the images, and sharing the images online? My research questions then became: (1) How do you experience selfies? (2) What do you gain from creating selfies?

I recruited four young women[2] aged between eighteen and thirty for this pilot project via purposive and snowball sampling. I approached female students at Kwantlen Polytechnic University, a teaching university in the culturally diverse suburb of Surrey, British Columbia, who had been taking selfies for more than two years and take more than three selfies per week. I also used snowball sampling to ask some participants to identify friends who also regularly took selfies.

Since phenomenological interviews seek the *lived experience* each interview is much more intense, longer, and rigorous, and involves diving into the lived and often poetic embodied experience of the participant. Before each interview I met with each participant to detail the difference between a qualitative interview and a phenomenological interview in order to encourage them to think about the lived embodied experience of selfie taking.[3]

The four young women I recruited represented an intersectionally diverse range in terms of culture, race, class, and family makeup and they offered the following demographic and character information to describe themselves. Nina[4] is nineteen. Her parents are Vietnamese refugees and were divorced when she was sixteen. Nina has a younger sister and she also lives with a cousin. She is a practicing Christian and she has a boyfriend. Jackie is a twenty-one-year-old Catholic female. She moved to Surrey in 2010 from Manila, Philippines and lives with her parents. Kelly is a twenty-four-year-old female of Canadian-Ukrainian heritage. She is agnostic and calls herself a modern-day hippie. She lives on her own and works part time to support herself independently through school. Kayla is a twenty-four-year-old female of Jamaican descent. She is an only child and describes herself as over analytical and a dreamer and a thinker. She lives with her parents.

I developed a variation of photo elicitation (Michael J. Emmison and Philip D. Smith 2000; Douglas A. Harper 2012; Caroline Knowles and Paul Sweetman 2004) and in-depth interviews to explore the lived experiences, feelings, and beliefs of the participants (Groenewald 2004; Hycner 1985). I was particularly interested in the feelings that emerged in the moment of image production. Douglas Harper discusses something akin to immediate photo-elicitation where the temporal gap between the image being taken, and the subject reflecting on the image is minimized so participants reflect freshly on the feelings and experiences associated with a given moment in time (Groenewald 2004; Hycner 1985). In a private interview room, I set up a digital video recorder on a desk and flipped the view-screen outward so the participant could see herself on the screen. I provided different lighting options (fluorescent overhead lights, lamps, and tripod mounted photo lighting). I then gave each young woman up to ten minutes to prepare the room and camera, as she desired.

I started by asking each young woman a series of questions from an interview guide[5] I had prepared that encouraged her to reflect on the phenomenon of taking selfies. These preliminary interviews lasted between forty-five minutes and one hour each. After the interview phase, I asked the young women to take as many selfies as they wanted until they produced two images they felt were good enough to share on a social media platform.[6] For the selfie-taking process, I asked each young woman to narrate freely and naturally her thoughts and feelings and the experience of taking, reviewing, editing, and applying filters to her selfies (Hycner 1985). Taking selfies is a discursively influenced practice[7] and as such, selfies are often taken in private locations (Katie Warfield 2015). Thus, I was out of the room, speaking with and watching the young women through Google™ chat as well as taking observational notes (Groenewald 2004). Although Google™ chat was set up and I could see them, I turned my camera off so that I wasn't visible to them. Further, I gave each young woman the option to have me step away from the computer while she actually took the photos, to lessen my influence on her process, and all four young women asked me to step out of the room. Upon leaving I asked them to narrate to the recording camera what they were feeling and thinking in the taking, editing, deleting, and selecting process. Once the selfie-taking stage was complete, I returned to the room and asked each young woman further reflexive questions about that exercise for another twenty–thirty minutes.

Mirror glitches

When the first cellphones with a front-facing camera were developed in 2003, a TV spot for the Sony Erikson z1010™ was produced which could be read as a post-phenomenologist's dream. With pulsing music playing in the background, the ad showed an animated high-tech assembly line producing the Erikson z1010™. At one point a black funnel is plugged into the screen of the device and one by one a camera, a laptop, dice (game), a bell (alarm), and a calendar are siphoned into the device.[8] The multi-stabilities of the cellphone were front and center in their marketing campaign.

One multi-stability that was not visualized in the ad, but was quite obvious in my empirical observation, was the cellphone-as-mirror. When the front-facing camera is turned on, it *reflects* in real-time, the face of the person taking the image. In the process of setting up the interview room to take photos, every one of the four young women used the cellphone as a mirror: to fluff hair, check out angles, and touch up makeup. Several theorists have observed and written about the extension of offline gender norms into the use of technologies including social media both in terms of adhering to gender norms (Alice E. Marwick 2015) and challenging them (Amy Shields Dobson 2013; Katrin Tiidenberg and Edgar Gomez-Cruz 2015).

With the cellphone-as-mirror, however, I want to posit that the mirror was used not simply to *look*, but rather to look, assess, and materially alter one's appearance through a form of material and discursively gendered form of *foreplay*. In the Glitch Manifesto, Russell (2012) describes the push and pull of this interaction:

> Though pejoratively dismissed all too frequently as an aspect of technical error, for me the glitch denotes an extension of the realm of foreplay whether it be "play" with oneself, or with virtualized other, imagined, or waiting just on the other side of the proverbial screen. (3)

In the initial moments of producing a selfie, there is usually a period of bodily and technological foreplay sparked by encounters with glitches. Nina called this the "warming up phase." She touched and arranged her hair reflecting on her appearance in the cellphone-as-mirror:

> I just showered so my hair is nice.

The glitches that appeared during the cellphone-as-mirror stability were *corporeal* and visibly gendered—glitches were identified on the skin (a blemish, a shadow), glitches of the hair (too flat, too big), and glitches on the body (misarranged shirt). In the moment of identifying the glitch the hand connected to, and materially smoothed out, these glitches on the body: Kayla looked at herself on the screen, pulled out her lipstick and re-applied the redness as if the cellphone were a pocket mirror or rearview mirror in a car.

Using the cellphone-as-mirror, Kelly decided at first glance that normally she wouldn't be taking a selfie at that moment based on her looks:

> And even today, probably I wouldn't normally be taking selfies because it's a bad hair day but, I'll make a sacrifice.

She then brushed her hair off her face, sucked in her cheeks, and opening her eyes wide, turned her head from side to side. I hold off from speculating the cause and effect relationship here between technology and self as if the technology *is causing* more self-reflection or analysis and further whether this is good or bad, rather, in a feminist new material sense, I try to observe the entanglements here and highlight how the young women discuss them: the technology is used to reflect on the body and aspects of the body (the hair), and play with one's physical features (cheeks, eyes), but the camera is intimately entangled in this and perhaps inseparable from it—the body and the technology dance as one in a techno-somatic entanglement. The image reflects. The body moves. The body moves. The image fluidly changes. This is less an interaction as it is an intra-action of the body and sense of self becoming along with and through the technology.

In this initial and early stage of foreplay, the cellphone is, what Wellner would call a wall—a flat and hard surface that mimics a mirror. The women arrange themselves as if alone, as if in solitude in front of a mirror. They arrange their hair, their faces, and their bodies playing with gendered tropes of self-presentation: pursed lips, head tilting, checking angles that make their faces looks "slim." Mirrors have often been used as either a metaphor or an actual tool (like a hand held mirror) for reflection upon the body/self relationship or *body-talk* (Nicole Landry Sault 1994). But the selfie is different because it is a mirror and a camera. The technology is used as an intimate device of self-reflection and self-presentation where corporeal glitches like misplaced hair and imperfect makeup are immediately managed and fixed, and in the moment of catered perfection snapped and preserved. In that moment of glitch, the presumed separation of body/body image is bridged.

Camera glitches

The second invariant of the cellphone that comprises the selfie is the cellphone-as-camera. When the front-facing camera took off with its incorporation in the IPhone4™, the advertisements for the device highlighted the camera function and aimed that function directly to female consumers. Particularly evident in the history of the Kodak Brownie™, women were tasked as the photographers or memory keepers of the heteronormative family unit (Kamal A. Munir and Nelson Phillips 2005). And this gendered relation to photography continues today. In a series of ads for the IPhone4 with Facetime between 2008 and 2011 we see: a young mom and her baby video-chatting with a dad who is away in a hotel room, seemingly on a work trip; two young female best friends, at separate colleges, facetime and ask each other advice on wardrobe options; a pregnant woman video chats from an ultrasound exam room with her partner away in the military.

For the group of young women I worked with, the cellphone-as-camera evoked a further form of gendered affective foreplay between technology, the screen, and the body:

Kayla: So I'm just trying to get the camera so that it's looking down more cause that definitely makes your face look thinner too. And then I always like suck my cheeks in, like (sucks in cheeks) … Like that so that…so that I don't know what that is but it looks good in pictures.

Kayla adopted gendered photographic tropes of the cellphone like those in the MySpace™ angle (Alice E. Marwick 2014, 2015; Lauren F. Sessions 2009). But on the other hand, Kelly actively worked against these tropes because they didn't work for her:

I know a lot of times the higher up selfie, from what I've heard anyways, people like doing it because if they are a little more self conscious with their body maybe it does make them look a little smaller which is the "idealistic" standards in media or whatever. But I mean I definitely try it, I don't try it thinking like if it doesn't turn out, I'm a loser. It's just in the sense that it doesn't hurt to try. If it works out great if it doesn't no harm, no foul no one is going to see it anyways.

In this phase the images are shaped to conform to and play within the domain of conventional representations of the female body in Western visual culture. The camera is not an inert technological agent here but encourages gendered forms of self representation, as it has historically demanded of the female subject before it (Luce Irigaray and Gillian C. Gill 1985). The young women played with the cellphone-as-camera often until finding what were deemed to be good angles, background, lighting, and facial expressions.

Although influenced by representational tropes, the desired photo, as described by the participants, could not be *just a photo*. In fact, the glitches that were identified by the group were the ones that made visible the technology, that made visible the cellphone-as-camera, and that made the photo too much a *typical* photo. When these glitches appeared, they too had to be ironed out or erased.

Jackie: So I'm going to adjust the lighting because I don't want my face to look super bright. Okay (*takes a photo, pauses*) humph. I don't like this first one because it's blurry. See it looks blurry? (*turns camera to the screen in her room to show me*). I like the second one more because I like how the light hits my face. Lighting is important. I usually like it more when my cheek bones look prominent. And if there's sort of a shadow at my jaw line.

For Jackie, with the cellphone-as-camera, the second set of glitches appeared on the surface of the *photos* as opposed to the surface of the *body* as was the case with the cellphone-as-mirror. These glitches included: blurriness, lighting, and poor angles. These glitches marked moments when the technology was *too visible*. The technology can never be too visible. It can't dominate. In this invariant, with the cellphone-as-camera, a good selfie is a *representation* of the self via technology not a presentation of the technology.

That said, the desired image was always in an entangled balance between a quality photo, but also not too much of a prototypical gendered representation of the self. When the image looked too posed, too much like (and only like) a *representation*, when the photos presented the young women too much like what the *camera* usually presents women as (flat objectified texts) then the selfies were tossed away.

Nina: Okay, I like the white background. Oh, that's so awkward. Like my smile is so not real! I don't like fake smiles. I like smiles like where you are in the middle of laughing, a more genuine type of smile.For Nina, a selfie is not just a photo. A photo is static, whereas a selfie has dynamism, affect, and authenticity. Jackie described a similar position:

Jackie: Sometimes I try to change my facial expression a bit but it doesn't work.

FEMINIST RECEPTION STUDIES IN A POST-AUDIENCE AGE

K: Why doesn't it work?

Jackie: Uh, it doesn't look like me. It doesn't feel real. I don't feel true to myself if I see it.

K: It doesn't feel real?

Jackie: Ya, I feel like sort of a poser.

What the participants sought were dimensions of *affective authenticity*. They drew on words like "real" and not "fake" but a new materialist analysis of authenticity complicates simple categories like real and fake. Although the participants played a lot with representational conventions, copying convention wasn't enough to make a good selfie. A good selfie was a combination of representationally gendered tropes and affective relationality—it had to look good but also *feel authentic*. According to glitch feminism (Russell 2012), glitches can help to reveal "such messy moments in gender, which simultaneously reveals the ghostly conventionality of gender norms and ideals, and the potentiality of a break with such conventions" (3). It is here in these moments where gender norms embedded in the technology of the camera are, via the glitch, shaped by the historical gendered invariants of the technology, performed by the body, and negotiated alongside the momentary and changing affectively felt sense of self which is also the result of a whole genealogy of material and discursive entanglements that have intra-actively made Nina who she is at that moment. We are not looking at interaction of entities, we are looking at a temporal complexity of material discursive entanglements.

Theorists of social media studies have examined and critiqued the concept of online self-presentation and authenticity (Raz Schwartz and Germaine R. Halegoua 2014). However, the concept of the authentic subject has been critiqued by theorists as a classic and humanistic trope that aligns *authenticity* with offline experiences and *inauthenticity* with online performance. Theorists of gender and sexuality have argued that the classic canon, and thus the contemporary concept of the "authentic self," is entwined with patriarchic theories of selfhood wherein authenticity signifies the linear development of the proper masculine subject (Silvia Stoller 2000) Jackie describes the paradox of online authenticity:

> Ya, like I want it to look natural, which is weird to say natural because I'm editing a picture. Which is kind of um, subjective because what I look like and what someone else thinks I look like could be totally different.

There are several ways to look at authenticity within a post-humanist or contemporary phenomenological approach that also allow us to think about both gender and subjectivity. Taking a feminist new materialist approach, which would reject an *a priori* subject who identifies with the entity of the image, the authenticity or "realness" is more a material discursive and affective entanglement that comes out of the moment of image making. It's not a matter of an essential self aligning with a image, rather, it's more an image and self that come about intra-actively from this specific entanglement where the body, gendered discourses, technologies work as an assemblage to yield the product of the good image of the momentary self. Neither discourses nor materiality are separate and preexisting entities, instead they are intimately entangled in that moment and within a genealogical material discourse history. The reconfiguring lies in the micro reconfigurations of what Barad (2007) calls *space–time–matterings* related to gender, or put simply, the mapping of genders as they normatively are. Authenticity could be seen as being related to having a final say in and reconfiguring one's representational form—even if that form is, to a degree (or entirely), a mediated material and discursive assemblage of gendered tropes.

The concept of authenticity begs more attention when we examine it through a lens of gender. In this quote, Nina doesn't just want to be a model in a picture—*that "doesn't feel real"*—she seeks to produce an expression of herself intra-actively through an affective and embodied quality of authenticity negotiated alongside the material image in front of her. The good image can never just be a pretty body. Rather it involves a picture with affect and punctum (Barthes and Howard 1982) that is an *entangled* negotiation of feeling, image, material body, and subjectivity. This primacy of affect in regards to the body image is suggestive of the work of Gayle Salamon who encourages us, via her major contribution to transgender theory, to rethink our assumptions about the primacy, fixedness, and accessibility of the materiality in theorizing the gendered body. She suggests that the lived experience of the body is most often felt as fragmented, multiple, changing, incomplete, in process, and in "bits and pieces" (33), whereas the *body image* permits a removed, somewhat distant (or very distant) projected dream of a unified stable embodied self. In other words, whereas more often the notion of the *body image* is seen as secondary and dependent on the assumed to be more *real* and *a priori* version of the material body, Salamon proposes a reversal, where we can also imagine the body image as *foundational and primary* and on which the materiality of the body may be redefined. Using the model alongside the selfie, then, it is not the body that is being changed by gendered discourses, but rather it is the affective feeling of the young woman in the image that is defining how the materiality of the body can be shifted, shaped, and reformed.

Social media glitches

The integration of popular photography apps took off in 2010 with the launch of Instagram™ as a free mobile app, Snapchat™ in 2011, and then the acquisition of Instagram™ by Facebook™ and Facebook's™ subsequent launch of its mobile app for IOS and Android. The final invariant, the cellphone-as-social-media-door completes the multi-stability trio of the invariants. The selfie is not just an *embodied* negotiation with a mirror, and not only a pure photographic *representation*: it is also self-presentation via the social media platform(s) on which it will be distributed.

Both Kayla and Kelly describe the importance of the imagined audiences of social media platforms as playing a role in shaping their selfies. As such then, within this final invariant, the glitches are located in the *typical ways these young women present themselves to different audiences on* different social media platforms. I use the term social media door to connote the spatiality of the social media platform as the young women discuss it. The social media platform is not flat but is experienced as a place or location. And different social media platforms are experienced as different types of places occupied by different audiences:

> Kayla: And I wouldn't use that one because one of my eyes looks a little small, and it looks a little angry and I wouldn't want people to think I am angry.

Kelly also describes the visual presentations of the self she wants, or doesn't want, her varied social media publics to see. She describes this when she is reviewing her photos:

> Kelly: It's a bit of a crapshoot when you decide to do goofy faces. There are definitely flattering goofy faces and then there's ones that you don't really want anyone to ever see. This one would definitely be one of them.

FEMINIST RECEPTION STUDIES IN A POST-AUDIENCE AGE

K: Why is that?

Kelly: Um, explaining why, I've got, well you can decide for yourself. I've got crazy eye going on. It's just something I wouldn't really want to share with other people so I'll delete that one.

Here were have an illustration of the increasingly gauzy borders between the stabilities of the multi-stability: "flattering-goofy faces" ride the line between cellphone-as-camera (since it needs to still look "flattering") but also illustrate personality and her persona ("goofy"). If it doesn't combine both, then she doesn't want her imagined audience (Hogan 2010) to see it.

The specificity of audience is also mentioned when it comes to selfies and the cellphone-as-social-media-door. What might be considered a glitch on one social media platform and to one audience, may be perfectly fine to share on a different social media platform with a different audience:

Nina: So that one's "okay." Like I would share that more over Snapchat but not over, maybe Instagram, but not Facebook. Facebook is more [of] a professional medium. Snapchat is more for when I'm bored like take a selfie with a super weird face and send it to someone. And then I'll draw on like a hat or something or a moustache.

The addition of a "hat" or a "moustache" in this final quote provides a final example of the multi-faceted glitching of the boundaries presumed to separate the corporeal body from the online self, the discursive from the material, and online from the offline. The "okay"-ness of the image of the body gives Nina ambivalence—the image as *affective*. What does the image *need* in order be shared? The body is a site of performativity (Judith Butler 1988) and here the image of the body isn't quite enough, to be shared, she suggests heightening certain visual elements to add a "weird"-ness to the image so the communicative intent—the image as *message*—is clearer. Here we see an entanglement of body, affect, representation, and audience. The audience is referenced again when Nina thinks about where the image will be distributed: Facebook is professional, Snapchat and Instagram may work but the image has to be made more playful—image as *performance*. The image, again, comes out of an *intra-action* with these multiple material discursive situations and Nina's specific corporeal, embodied, representational, and presentational experiences.

Selfie as MirrorCameraDoor

Increasingly as the young women got close to capturing an image to share online, the toggling between multi-stable technologies became blurry and the selfie became a unified assemblage of the interactions with at once the cellphone-as-mirror, the cellphone-as-camera, and the cellphone-as-window. Once all the glitches that visibly delineated one invariant from the next were removed, the selfie was approved:

Nina: If my smile is too forced, or out of focus I'm not going to use it later. Like this one. No I don't like it. I like being in focus (*reviews photos*). Okay, this one we can keep. It's more normal. It's a bit forced but more a natural forced. It's kind of awkward but it's okay (*reviews photos*). There! This one! I like this one because I think that's what I am. It's a bit eccentric. And the hair is just perfect like part of it just sits here (*reviews photos*). Okay I think I got two that I like. So this is the one. I like this one because I think it's me. It's a bit crazy and cooky and I think it's what I am. And I think I can be really hyper. And I like this one because it's more normal. It's like "hi I'm shy" and it's not as forced. I'm going to delete the rest of them.\

In the end, what we see is not a multi-stable toggling between clearly defined and bounded stabilites: the mirror, then camera, then social media door. Instead we see the multi-stable bridging that marks the good selfie: the smile is not too forced, and so the photo is not too much of a staged photo (representation). The hair is perfect, and so it fits with the corporeally shaped private self put together in front of the cellphone-as-mirror (embodiment). But the photo also visually reveals qualities of Nina's personality (presentation): "It's bit crazy and cooky and I think it's what I am." The good image can be seen as a crossing of axes—where the image presents the corporeal self (embodiment), the curated self (representation), and the social media self (presentation) in a situated, and concurrent online and offline series of places and moments.

There were limitations to this study. Selfies are typically taken in environments like bedrooms, cars, and bathrooms; as such the manufactured nature of the interview is a limitation. The benefit of this method, however, was the ability to record in real-time the selfie-taking process. As far as I could find, there does not exist an app, which can simultaneously video record in the background while someone takes a photos. Further, the sample size of four in-depth interviews is not generalizable but this study is positioned as a pilot, which I plan to conduct anew in 2017 with a larger sample of participants. Further, the aim was not generalizability but rather to be descriptive and focused on the experiential. The findings do, however, contribute some insight into the specific cohort of avid selfie takers, which is a specific population of users.

There are several questions for further inquiry. Given Ihde's (2012) work with the notion of embodiment technologies, it would be interesting to look at a qualitative longitudinal study of selfie-taking practices: do technologies become increasingly enfolded under the skin over time? Increasingly habitual and glitch-free?

Conclusion

I began this paper by presenting a pilot study of interviews and a novel approach to photo-elicitation to explore the lived experiences of four young intersectionally diverse young women who regularly take and share selfies via social media. What this paper shows is how, in the process of producing a selfie, the cellphone is experienced by this group of young women, as a *multi-stable* technological phenomenon (Ihde 2012): meaning it comprises three invariants: a mirror, a camera, and a door to social media platforms. This paper extends the work of post-phenomenological theorists like Wellner (2016) and supports her claim that the cellphone as a multi-stable technology could have many axes and many plateaus. Not simply as a wall and window (as Wellner [2016] suggests) but much more nuanced based on the multiple and varied functions of the cellphone all of which may yield different phenomenological experiences to diverse users. I further suggest that, contrary to what Wellner (2016) proposes, the everyday encounters with these stabilities *are* experienced as gendered—as the young women in this study experienced themselves in front of the mirror and camera and subsequently played with and through gendered tropes of the presentation of the body and so it is important not to bracket power dynamics from post-phenomenological analyses.

This paper encourages a rethinking of other categories too—particularly those that often guide work in audience research, as I mentioned at the start, like producer, medium, audience. Here the producer (the image taker) is not a bounded entity but is an entanglement herself: of body, affect, gender, which themselves are further complex entanglements. For instance, the camera is not just a benign technology but also a material interface set within an entangled genealogy of gendered discourses. The audience is both real and imagined, as well as both online and offline, and further embodied within the psyche of the image taker. This is not a model of clear cause and effect at all. It is a model of fluidity, complexity, change, becoming, and responsibility comprising material and discursive forces in the moment, and genealogically ossified.

Glitch feminism is of particular help in cracking the boundaries between entities like body/technology and online/offline. In this paper, I have posited that the glitches in this phenomenon occur in both material and discursive as well as online and offline locations and, as such, work to hiccup the boundaries between these entities. I propose that we think about glitches as binary-punctuating agents in the material-discursive production of the selfie. I suggest we think about glitches—on the body, the image, and the social-media performance—as Russell (2012) pitched as "a little digital death, a wheeze, a shift, a breath, a sneeze, a pause […] that breaks down *digital dualism*: and reconnects the online from the offline, the image from the body" (1). With a new materialist attitude, I suggest the glitches in these selfies be, as Russell proposes, not the *errors*, but in fact the *catalyst* that runs a plank between the offline affective body and the socially mediated experiential self and permits us to explore our deepest desires (Russell 2012, 4).

Glitch feminism provides a fruitful in-road to studying the visuality of gender online, "and the revolutionary role the digital practice has in expanding the construction, deconstruction, and re-presentation of the female-identifying corpus" (Sundén 2015, 5). As Sundén (2015) reminds us: "Glitch is rarely a complete collapse of the machinery. The machine is still running, but the performance is poor" (3). Glitches serve to remind us of the transparency and power of technologies, as well as their manufactured and thus breakable nature. This does not mean that gender is completely collapsed but rather drawing on the work of Gayle Salamon (2010) I suggest the importance of the affective self in the construction of gender. Salamon's notion that the body is "radically particular" and further that that affective sense of self is changing and more fluid as the group of young women I worked with sought a multitude of different "selves" that differed based on rubbing up against different people, interfaces, places, and technologies.

What this paper hopefully illustrates is that authenticity and play are not mutually exclusive when the self is implicitly multiple, dependent on, and emerging in different discursive and material entanglements. In a medium that is multi-stable (the cellphone), the self is therefore *always multiple*, layered, fluid, and changing. Perhaps a rethinking of authenticity is in order and rather than a humanist notion that aligns with the notion of the *real* we may consider a post-human authenticity that draws on the etymological origins of authenticity that connect to concepts of "authoring" and "writing." Through a post-human feminist new materialism lens, perhaps what these young women are doing is, via the entanglement of producer, text, and audience, affectively writing into being, via the selfie, their post-human body-selves—which are not and never have been essential or singular but rather are complex entanglement of flesh, technology, discourse, materiality, past, and present. Perhaps the authenticity these young women seek is a transient assemblage of authorship: it's a push and pull.

Notes

1. In this paper I define the term "phenomenon" not in the phenomenological sense but rather in a feminist new materialist sense, which sees phenomena as material-discursive ontological entanglements (Barad 2007).
2. Although a sample size of four seems small for typical qualitative interviews, for phenomenological data collection, which is the orientation of in-depth interview on which my interviews were modeled (Thomas Groenewald 2004; Richard H. Hycner 1985) suggested sample size is typically more than two but less than ten.
3. These pre-meetings added between one to two hours to each interview session. I should note too that this project was aimed to be a pilot project for future research and I am presently repeating the research and refining the methods with another group of ten participants.
4. All names of participants are pseudonyms.
5. I provide some of the questions from the interview later in this paper.
6. I did not ask them to post the images online.
7. The discursive treatment of selfies has been examined by several theorists including Anne Burns (2015) and Theresa Senft and Nancy Baym (2015).
8. https://www.youtube.com/watch?v=x04eVDn2dN4.

Disclosure statement

No potential conflict of interest was reported by the author.

References

Barad, Karen. 2007. *Meeting the Universe Halfway: Quantum Physics and the Entanglement of Matter and Meaning*, 2nd edn. Durham, NC: Duke University Press.
Barthes, Roland, and Richard Howard. 1982. *Camera Lucida: Reflections on Photography*. New York: Hill and Wang.
Bird, Elizabeth. 2003. *The Audience in Everyday Life: Living in a Media World*. London, England: Routledge.
Braidotti, Rosi. 2001. *Metamorphoses: Towards a Materialist Theory of Becoming*. Cambridge, England: Polity Press.
Burns, Anne. 2015. "Selfies: Self(ie)-Discipline: Social Regulation as Enacted Through the Discussion of Photographic Practice." *International Journal of Communications* 9: 1716–1733.
Butler, Judith. 1988. "Performative Acts and Gender Constitution: An Essay in Phenomenology and Feminist Theory." *Theatre Journal* 40 (4): 519. doi:10.2307/3207893.
Deuze, Mark. 2012. *Media Life*. Cambridge: John Wiley and Sons.
Dobson, Amy Shields. 2013. Performative Shamelessness on Young Women's Social Networks Sites: Shielding the Self and Resisting Gender Melancholia. *Feminism & Psychology*, February, 24 (1), 97–114.
Dolphijn, Rick, and Iris van der Tuin. 2012. *New Materialism: Interviews and Cartographies*. Ann Arbor, MI: Open Humanities Press.
Emmison, Michael J., and Philip D. Smith. 2000. *Researching the Visual: Images, Objects, Contexts and Interactions in Social and Cultural Inquiry*. London, England: Sage.

FEMINIST RECEPTION STUDIES IN A POST-AUDIENCE AGE

Fahringer, Karl, and Axel Bruns. 2008. *Blogs, Wikipedia, Second Life, and Beyond: From Production to Produsage*. New York: Peter Lang Publishing.

Farman, Jason. 2014. *Mobile Interface Theory: Embodied Space and Locative Media*. New York: Routledge.

Goffman, Erving. 1974. *The Presentation of Self in Everyday Life*. New York: Overlook Press.

Groenewald, Thomas. 2004. "A Phenomenological Research Design Illustrated." *International Journal of Qualitative Methods* 3 (1), Article 4.

Harper, Douglas A. 2012. *Visual Sociology: An Introduction*. New York: Taylor and Francis.

Heidegger, Martin, and William Lovitt. 1978. *The Question Concerning Technology: And Other Essays*. New York: Facsimiles-Garl.

Hillis, Ken, Susanna Paasonen, and Michael Petit, eds. 2015. *Networked Affect*. Cambridge, MA: MIT Press.

Hogan, Bernie. 2010. "The Presentation of Self in the Age of Social Media: Distinguishing Performances and Exhibitions Online." *Bulletin of Science, Technology & Society* 30: 377–386.

Hycner, Richard H. 1985. "Some Guidelines for the Phenomenological Analysis of Interview Data." *Human Studies* 8 (3): 279–303. doi:10.1007/bf00142995.

Ihde, Don. 2012. *Experimental Phenomenology: Multistabilities*. Albany, NY: Suny Press.

Irigaray, Luce, and Gillian C. Gill. 1985. *Speculum of the Other Woman*, 3rd edn. Ithica, NY: Cornell University Press.

Jurgensen, Nathan. 2011. "Digital Dualism and the Fallacy of Web Objectivity." *The Society Pages*, September 13. http://thesocietypages.org/cyborgology/2011/09/13/digital-dualism-and-the-fallacy-of-web-objectivity/

Knowles, Caroline, and Paul Sweetman. 2004. *Picturing the Social Landscape: Visual Methods and the Sociological Imagination*. London, England: Taylor and Francis.

Lasén, Amparo, and Edgar Gómez-Cruz. 2009. "Digital Photography and Picture Sharing: Redefining the Public/Private Divide." *Knowledge, Technology and Policy* 22 (3): 205–215. doi:10.1007/s12130-009-9086-8.

Lewis, Justin. 2013. *The Ideological Octopus: An Exploration of Television and Its Audience*. New York: Routledge Libraries Edition: Television.

Livingstone, Sonia, and Ranjana Das. 2009. "The End of Audiences? Paper presented at: Theoretical Echoes of Reception amid the Uncertainties of Use." *Transforming audiences 2*, University of Westminster, 3-4 September 2009. (Unpublished).

Marwick, Alice E. 2014. *Status Update: Celebrity, Publicity, and Branding in the Social Media Age*. New Haven, CT: Yale University Press.

Marwick, Alice E. 2015. "Instafame: Luxury Selfies in the Attention Economy." *Public Culture* 27 (1): 137–160. doi:10.1215/08992363-2798379.

Munir, Kamal A., and Nelson Phillips. 2005. "The Birth of the 'Kodak Moment': Institutional Entrepreneurship and the Adoption of New Technologies." *Organization Studies* 26 (11): 1665–1687. doi:10.1177/0170840605056395.

Oxford English Dictionary. 2015. s.v "Selfie."

Rettberg, Jill Walker. 2014. *Seeing Ourselves through Technology: How We Use Selfies, Blogs and Wearable Devices to See and Shape Ourselves*. London, England: Palgrave Pivot.

Ringrose, Jessica, and Emma Renold. 2014. "'F**k Rape!': Exploring Affective Intensities in a Feminist Research Assemblage." *Qualitative Inquiry* 20 (6): 772–780. doi:10.1177/1077800414530261.

Russell, Legacy. 2012. "Digital dualism and the Glitch manifesto." *The Society Pages: Cybogology*, December 10. https://thesocietypages.org/cyborgology/2012/12/10/digital-dualism-and-the-glitch-feminism-manifesto/

Salamon, G. 2010. *Assuming a body: Transgender and rhetorics of materiality*. New York: Columbia University Press.

Sault, Nicole Landry. 1994. *Many Mirrors: Body Image and Social Relations*. New Jersey: Rutgers University Press.

Schwartz, Raz. and Germaine R. Halegoua. 2014. "The Spatial Self: Location-based Identity Performance on Social Media." *New Media and Society*, April 9: 1643–1660. doi: 10.1177/1461444814531364

Senft, Theresa M. 2015. "The Skin of the Selfie." In *Ego Update: The Future of Digital Identity*, edited by Alain Bieber. Dusseldorf, NRW: Forum Publications.

Senft, Theresa, and Nancy Baym. 2015. "What Does the Selfie Say? Investigating a Global Phenomenon." *International Journal of Communications* 9: 1588–1606.

Sessions, Lauren F. 2009. "'You Looked Better on MySpace': Deception and Authenticity on the Web 2.0." *First Monday* 14 (7). doi:10.5210/fm.v14i7.2539.

Stoller, Silvia. 2000. "Reflections on Feminist Merleau-Ponty Skepticism." *Hypatia* 15 (1): 175–182. doi:10.1111/j.1527-2001.2000.tb01084.x.

Sundén, Jenny. 2015. "On Trans-, Glitch, and Gender as Machinery of Failure." *First Monday* 20 (4): doi:10.5210/fm.v20i4.5895.

Tiidenberg, Katrin, and Edgar Gomez-Cruz. 2015. Selfies, Image and Remaking the Body. *Body & Society*. December 21 (4): 77–102.

Toffler, Alvin. 1980. *The Third Wave*. New York: William Morrow and Company.

Vorderer, Peter, and Matthias Kohring. 2013. "Permanently Online: A Challenge for Media and Communication Research." *International Journal of Communication* 7: 188–196.

Warfield, Katie. 2015. "The Model, the #realme, and the Self-Conscious Thespian: Digital Subjectivities in the Selfie." *International Journal on the Image* 6 (2): 1–16.

Wellner, Galit P. 2016. *A Postphenomenological Inquirt of Cellphones*. London, England: Lexington Books.

Fifty shades of consent?

Francesca Tripodi

ABSTRACT

Fifty Shades of Grey—often classified as "mommy porn"—is far from a joke when considering its widespread cultural appeal. The trilogy populated the *New York Times* bestseller list for months and also influenced the sexual entertainment industry. Given its prominence, scholars have sought to understand audiences' connection to the series, finding that *Fifty Shades* fans are using the narrative to navigate the post-feminist realities of hook-up culture. In this paper, I argue that existing research on audience engagement with *Fifty Shades* could go further since these studies are geared toward an audience largely crafted by marketers (heterosexual women who do not practice BDSM in their relationships). Using ethnographic observations and interviews inside a bondage, discipline, and sadomasochism (BDSM) community, I argue that since *Fifty Shades* continues to frame BDSM as a stigma, it obscures the important ways that BDSM communities work to create a culture of active consent. This is problematic because if audiences are turning to books like *Fifty Shades* as a form of "self-help," as post-feminist scholars suggest, *Fifty Shades* ultimately reifies the fact that consent, negotiation, and communication remain unexamined topics in "vanilla" versions of sex and love.

Introduction

The *Fifty Shades* trilogy—a series of erotic romance novels chronicling the relationship between Anastasia Steele (Ana) and Christian Grey—is a cultural phenomenon. Written by E.L. James as a fan-fiction spinoff of *Twilight*, *Fifty Shades* has sold more than one-hundred-million copies worldwide and spent over one hundred weeks on the *New York Times* bestseller list (Julie Bosman 2014). Raking in over $81 million during Valentines weekend, the film adaptation broke box office records. To date it is the highest-grossing Presidents Day weekend opener and ranks among the highest R-rated releases in history (Brent Lang 2015).

The series gained notoriety because of its frequent, and rather explicit, erotic scenes featuring BDSM practices that subsequently caused an uptick in sex-toy sales. For example, in the first book of the *Fifty Shades* series, a pair of "Ben Wa Balls" are used by Christian to sexually arouse Ana during a familial dinner party. The company that manufactures the balls reported that prior to the release of *Fifty Shades of Grey* the company sold between eighty- and ninety-thousand per year and after the book's initial debut, the company sold one million in six months (Rachel Abrams 2015). In conjunction with the release of the movie, many erotic stores modified their inventory to include movie tie-ins and direct marketing. Babeland, one of the leading adult toy retailers online, now includes a separate subcategory under Bondage called "Fifty Shades of Grey" which drives consumers to merchandise like the "Red Room Blindfold," an "Ultimate Control Hand Cuff Set," or the "Ultimate Date Night Set."[1]

Given its cultural prominence, scholars have sought to better understand how, and why, audiences are so invested in the series. Drawing on the work of feminist cultural studies, researchers argue that rather than a longing to be "dominated," readers are using *Fifty Shades* as a way of guiding them through the post-feminist milieu in which they are currently living. Specifically, they argue that since women's sexual knowledge and prowess can serve as a form of empowerment but also cause relationship problems, women are using the series as a way of navigating relationship uncertainties (Melissa Click 2015; Eva Illouz 2014). This runs contradictory to the harsh criticisms *Fifty Shades* has received in mainstream media and the blogosphere where many argue that the relationship portrayed in *Fifty Shades* is akin to intimate-partner violence.[2] However, similar to Janice Radway's (1984) research on why audiences read romance novels, *Fifty Shades* fans aren't longing for an abusive relationship—rather they are turning to books like *Fifty Shades* as a way of dealing with the problems of misogyny they face in their everyday lives.

While this important feminist scholarship challenges criticisms of *Fifty Shades*, I argue it focuses too narrowly on what constitutes "an audience" and therefore fails to engage with what might be *missing* from the *Fifty Shades* narrative. To fill this gap, I conducted ethnographic observations, interviews, and focus groups with individuals who participate in BDSM communities. My research reveals that while *Fifty Shades* accurately includes some BDSM buzzwords (i.e., contracts or safe words) how they are *used* within BDSM relationships is misguided. I argue that because *Fifty Shades* excludes these imperative aspects of BDSM relationships, James ultimately reifies a heteronormative standard whereby silence means yes when it comes to agreeing to participate in sexual acts. By exploring a prominent disjuncture between the "*Safe, Sane, Consensual*" mantra of BDSM culture with a media portrayal of BDSM life, I argue that while some forms of sexual agency might occur among heterosexual women in monogamous relationships, *Fifty Shades*' portrayal of BDSM obscures from readers an outlet that could help single women still navigating "hook-up" culture combat the persistent problem of non-consensual sex.

Fifty shades of self help

A myriad of researchers have demonstrated that women engage with traditionally female forms of media as a form of protest, rather than acceptance of, patriarchal culture (Liesbet van Zoonen 1994).[3] Similar to the work of Angela McRobbie, Dorothy Hobson, and/or Mary Ellen Brown, feminist cultural scholars looked specifically at how romance novels provide agency and value to women's voices. Carol Thurston (1987) found that women consciously use romance novels to project their own sexual fantasies. By imagining themselves in the same sexual situations that heroines face, romance novels afford women the opportunity to learn and try new kinds of sex thereby opening the doors for increased sexual pleasure. Since romance novels provide a conduit for readers to explore their own sexual agency, Thurston argues that romance novels foster, rather than undermine, feminist ideology.

FEMINIST RECEPTION STUDIES IN A POST-AUDIENCE AGE

Radway (1984) does not make the same evaluative claims, but rather finds that readers of romance novels (heterosexual women) strongly identify with the female heroines. Moreover, she finds that women are not reading the novels because they *share* misogynistic views. Rather, romance novel readers turn to fiction as a way of navigating and dealing with the patriarchal situations they live in. Specifically, she describes how housewives use romance novels as a way of carving out quiet time and personal space. By distancing them from their familial duties, reading the books served as a form of resistance as well as pleasure.

More recent scholastic work has looked specifically at the *Fifty Shades* series, and why it has such a strong cultural appeal. While Illouz (2014) does not draw from active audience methodology, she uses feminist cultural studies to argue that *Fifty Shades* acts more as a "self help" book for women searching for intimacy in an era when sexuality and empowerment are more closely aligned with consumerist (neoliberal) ideals than with romance. Illouz's theory—that *Fifty Shades* provides women with a text enabling them to navigate cultural expectations that women be sexual but not domineering—draws parallels to the challenges women face while maintaining a "postfeminist sensibility" (Rosalind Gill 2007). Specifically, Illouz argues that since women's sexual prowess is both an identity and a problem all at once, the very act of reading *Fifty Shades* feels like "self-improvement"—the reader can learn how to be a better and more fulfilled sexual partner while expressing her sexuality in a non-threatening way. Again, drawing on post-feminist theory, *Fifty Shades* allows women to express feminism "with a wink" (Susan Douglas 2010). Since empowerment in a post-feminist era requires women to both learn how to excite men while simultaneously relinquishing power, reading *Fifty Shades* thereby acts as a form of sexual autonomy (Illouz 2014).

In the tradition of active audience research, Click (2015) also argues that women turn to *Fifty Shades* as a way of understanding and navigating post-feminist sexualized culture. Drawing from interviews with thirty-six women, Click finds that fan engagement with *Fifty Shades* is less about wanting to be "dominated" and more about a personal reflection on their own sexual experiences in romantic relationships with men. Looking specifically at how female readers differentiate between the "lovemaking" (traditional bedroom sex) and the "fucking" scenes (BDSM), Click suggests that female audiences use *Fifty Shades* as a way of "making sense" of the sexual environment that has been changing in the late twentieth and early twenty-first centuries. In an environment where casual, non-dating sex, or "hooking up" has become the new standard, women need to adjust their sexual standards and expectations (2015, 17). Click argues that *Fifty Shades* provides a context by which women can help make sense of the sexualized culture in which they are immersed. My own preliminary audience research with self-described fans of *Fifty Shades*[4] echoes Click's findings: I found that women who read the book do not want to be dominated but rather used the series to explore their own sexual identity. Since the book is so sexual, it opened up the opportunity for readers to talk about sex with their friends and become more active sexual agents within existing relationships (primarily, in the case of my research, their heterosexual marriages).

This research sheds light on concepts that textual analysis alone could not provide. Both Illouz and Click make powerful arguments regarding how the use and interpretation of gendered media texts allow audiences to produce their own meanings within their existing cultural frameworks. While they provide an important start to understanding how a book like *Fifty Shades* can help navigate the persistence of patriarchy in a post-feminist era, I argue that research on *Fifty Shades,* and romance novels more broadly, continues to define the audience/readers of these novels as female, primarily heterosexual, and not engaged with "alternative" forms of sexuality.[5] Yet previous active audience researchers demonstrate that the very nature of "an audience" is fluid and does not fit neatly within institutionally defined boxes (Ien Ang 1991), particularly for a cultural product like *Fifty Shades* that is itself so indefinite and pervasive as a book, a film, a consumer good, and a topic for online forms. Cultural background, socioeconomic status, gender, race, among other factors all interact to influence how audiences engage, interpret, and identify with various media forms (Tamar Liebes and Elihu Katz 1990; Andrea Press 1991). This paper aims to fill this scholastic absence by understanding how readers (both men and women) who practice BDSM within their relationships interact and engage with *Fifty Shades*. By opening up the idea of a "Fifty Shades audience" to include women *and men* who both practice BDSM and do not identify exclusively as heterosexual, these findings also provide a voice for those frequently marginalized from scholastic inquiry.

Doing so subsequently provides an opportunity to push back on the idea that the book helps women navigate persistent patriarchal oppressions within hook-up culture, specifically when we consider the persistent problem of cultivating consent. Take the recent data provided by the Association of American Universities: sexual assault, in many different forms, is so widespread on American college campuses that by the time they graduate, 39.0 percent of females and 7.6 percent of males report being a victim of non-consensual sexual contact at least once. Perhaps more alarming is that over 50 percent of even the most serious cases of assault do not report the incident because they do not consider it "serious enough."[6] Given the pervasiveness of non-consensual experiences within hook-up culture, it is clear that women, and men, need help cultivating a more prolific "yes means yes" attitude when it comes to sexual experimentation, particularly when women must maintain some elements of traditional femininity (i.e., less confrontational and less domineering) while simultaneously exhibiting their sexual prowess. Data demonstrate that conversations about consent are clearly not happening. As a result we must question if narratives being used as a form of self-help, like *Fifty Shades*, are providing a space for women and men to discuss both their sexual desires *and* safely articulate their limits.

The study: expanding what constitutes the *Fifty Shades* "audience"

Similar to the gay and lesbian community formation in the late 1970s, those who practice BDSM have formed "quasi-ethnic, nucleated, sexually constituted communities" that include "a self-conscious identity, group solidarity, literature, and institutional structure" (Gayle Rubin 1984, 156), and these community enclaves exist both on and offline (Meg Barker 2013; Eleanor Wilkinson 2009). During the summer of 2013, I attended monthly meetings and local "munches" (casual social gatherings for people involved or interested in BDSM) with a BDSM community located in a city in the United States. During that same time period, I joined online BDSM community forums where I posted a call for interviews and set up a profile to conduct virtual ethnography.

In addition to my fieldwork, I also conducted ten semi-structured interviews and one focus group with individuals who were currently involved in a BDSM relationship. Five interviews (three men and two women) were conducted with individuals who participated in the community where I conducted my physical ethnographic observations. The remaining five interviews (all women) were recruited from online forums and conducted via Skype. The ages of the respondents ranged from nineteen to seventy with varying levels of education.

Two of the men interviewed identified as heterosexual and one identified as bisexual. Three of the women were currently in heterosexual relationships although identified as bisexual, half of the signal woman identified as heterosexual and half identified as bisexual.

A striking observation from my ethnographic observations was the limited racial diversity both within the physical group and online. Only one person interviewed identified as a racial minority (Latina). There was also limited socioeconomic diversity. While group members had a variety of jobs, it was clear from my observations and interviews that monetary constraints limit some from participating fully in BDSM practices.[7]

Relying on grounded theory, I used comparative distinctions (Kathy Charmaz 2006), the data were coded for similarities and differences that emerged from the interviews compared to that which was observed in the field. After flagging particularly salient *"in vivo* codes" (Charmaz Charmaz 2006), I then conducted a more focused coding, determining the accuracy of the threads identified. Using these themes, I compared my findings to existing research on *Fifty Shades*, the original *Fifty Shades* text and film adaptation, and popular press surrounding the *Fifty Shades* phenomenon.

Interest and identity: exploring why so many were drawn to *Fifty Shades*

In the same way that self-described fans were drawn to *Fifty Shades* because everyone was reading it (Click 2015), respondents in this study were also intrigued by the popularity of the series. Respondents who worked in adult entertainment stores wanted to see why so many new clients had come searching for *Fifty Shades* merchandise while others I interviewed wanted to understand why so many of their loved ones were reading the books. Since the series claimed to represent such a key aspect of their life, respondents wanted to know what had gotten such a large swath of the United States curious about BDSM. As Emma,[8] a young woman finishing up college in the Midwest, described

> I look around and my aunt is reading it and my cousin is reading it and like, that's kinda weird because I know that I'm for sure into this and I know what you're talking about and I know for sure that you don't. But all they have to go off is what it says in the book.

This enhanced curiosity about BDSM also created the need to set up increased boundary management within the community where I conducted my ethnographic observations because members had noticed new people coming to their meetings after reading *Fifty Shades*. An influx of new members was also occurring on the virtual sites, as one respondent described "but especially since *Fifty Shades*, there is a separate faction that has started to come up that I've noticed. People are starting to come in with no idea what it's about except for what they read from the book." In an effort to educate novice members, the group that I observed during the summer conducted a "safe practices" scenario at the beginning of one of their meetings. They marketed it as a refresher, but in talking with members after the meeting, they described a need to provide more information to new members whom they felt were not particularly educated in safe BDSM practices.[9]

It was this limited vision of their culture that respondents found so frustrating. As Kristy described: *Fifty Shades* was "very black and white" with very few "shades of grey" when it came to exploring BDSM. Veronica, a woman in her mid-twenties who works in an adult store and identifies as a submissive in her current relationship, expanded on the cultural distance she felt between her life and what she read in *Fifty Shades*:

> What's so infuriating in this book is this character that I'm supposed to identify with who is refusing to stand up for herself and refuses to be a human being and tell him it's not ok for you to stalk me, it's not ok for you to do these things that are getting into inappropriate abuse territory.

Or, as Jen, a new mother in her thirties explained of how James' wrote about the use of handcuffs in the books:

> that would never happen because metal handcuffs would hurt a lot. I personally don't know anyone who is into metal handcuffs, I've never seen them at a play party, they hurt. And that whole time the way he had her tied up in the scene I was like, there is no way they are using metal handcuffs she'd be in so much pain right now, she would be calling a stop to the scene.

Time and again, BDSM respondents stressed that the physical practices James authored could inflict injury and none of the submissives interviewed identified with Ana's character. In addition to physical harm by toys, many were also concerned about Christian's desire to isolate Ana. Mike, Jen's husband, was particularly disturbed that the characters met alone without others knowing their whereabouts:

> If you've never played with them before and they are going to come meet you or you're going to go meet them you let someone else from within the community know where you're going. Then you're supposed to call that person in an hour and if they don't call you, you call them and if they don't answer, you call again, you call again, and you call again and if they don't answer you call the cops.

BDSM respondents argue that these inaccuracies stem from the fact that James failed to engage with the practices she sought to represent. Given her cultural distance, it makes sense why, according to interviewees, she so inaccurately portrayed the submissive as powerless and failed to engage with a cornerstone of BDSM culture: "Safe, Sane, Consensual."

Submissive power: "people don't realize how consensual it is. They think that poor submissive without knowing they are in control" (Zoe)

One of the most glaring inconsistencies between *Fifty Shades* and my observations and interviews was how *Fifty Shades* portrayed the role of the submissive as relatively powerless. Take, for example, the language in the contract, which was framed around the "needs" of the dominant. While the dominant is expected to train the submissive and keep her safe, ensuring the *pleasure* of the submissive is not part of the agreement. Yet one of the first stipulations under submissive acts is that she must "serve the Dominant in any way the Dominant sees fit and shall endeavor to please the Dominant at all times to the best of her ability" (E.L. James 2011, 170). This is in stark contrast to my interviews and observations where I learned that submissives tend to have *more power* in the negotiation, because they are the ones who are receiving the pain. Moreover, dominants interviewed described it as their responsibility to given their submissive pleasure and it is typically the submissive who picks out what toys to use and the threshold of pain. The power of the submissive in a BDSM relationship is also recognized in a series of essays published in 2008 in the book *Yes Means Yes*. Specifically Stacy May Fowles (2008) and Lee Jacobs Riggs (2008) argue that submissives are often able to "find power" through domination because they are deeply engaged in the negotiation process through which they articulate their sexual desires. One submissive described how a scene works:

> It's more like, I know what is going to happen I just don't know when it's going to happen—and then of course you can stop at any time, but either person could do that. (Veronica)

FEMINIST RECEPTION STUDIES IN A POST-AUDIENCE AGE

By contrast, Christian is extremely domineering and does not take much of what Ana has to say into consideration. Moreover BDSM respondents were concerned about how much control Christian exercised on their relationship outside of scene play. While respondents acknowledged that they knew of some couples who are in 24/7 BDSM relationships, Christian did not comply with Ana's own needs for personal space, putting his own desires before hers. In this way, many BDSM participants see the book as more of a "vanilla" (i.e., heteronormative) sexual fantasy where men control women, rather than a narrative giving women the possibility to assert sexual authority and deviate from stereotypical gender tropes. As one woman, currently involved in a relationship as the submissive explained:

> The fact that he gets her jobs and a car and a computer is weird and unhealthy because my personal experience is that if I have a BDSM relationship with someone, that's the only power they have over me. Other than that we're just two people, two equals, they're not my employer, they're not particularly older than me, or particularly more wealthy, or anything that gives them a huge power advantage. It's just like we're two people, not like you're also my boss and I have to make you happy or I won't have a job. (Meredith)

Ana is expected to be "nice" and defer to Christian in sexual interaction. These expectations are strikingly similar to the norms observed by Elizabeth Armstrong, Laura Hamilton and Brian Sweeney (2006) in their study of how interaction facilitates instances of sexual assault on college campuses. The expectation that a guest reciprocates with sex is intensified by men's position as hosts and women's position as grateful guests (Armstrong, Hamilton, and Sweeney 2006), *Fifty Shades* further amplifies a situation whereby Ana is routinely put into a subordinate position of power. This is problematic when one considers that uneven power dynamics contribute to men's ability to control sexual strategies and mitigate the risk of engaging in non-consensual sex (Armstrong, Hamilton, and Sweeney 2006). Not unlike social situations that contribute to the persistence of non-consensual sex, alcohol (provided by Christian) is always involved when Christian and Ana meet; Ana is expected to be more provocatively dressed than Christian (especially since he purchases most of her wardrobe); she is expected to be grateful for his hospitality and gifts (indeed Christian often demands thanks for his generosity); and there is a significant power differential with regard to wealth, age, and sexual expertise (Christian is a twenty-six-year-old billionaire while Ana is a recent college graduate who is still a virgin when she meets Christian). Christian ultimately controls more than just the bedroom dynamics but also controls when and how she is able to leave his home. Portraying "submissives" in this way strips Ana of agency rather than giving her the power over her sexual encounters, which BDSM respondents describe as central to a submissive's role.

In this way, Ana isn't really being a submissive because it is something that she wants to do but rather she's doing it to *please* someone else. Submissives I interviewed were particularly perturbed by this depiction of the submissive as powerless and felt that Ana did not really seem to enjoy being submissive—as Jen described:

> I was surprised when I found out that there was a second and a third one. I was like, why are there more books? She tested out this lifestyle and realized she didn't like it—what is going on here?

Ana's desire to please Christian more than herself made some respondents concerned that people new to BDSM might try it just to maintain a relationship, rather than for their own pleasure. In this way, *Fifty Shades* promotes "conservative feminism" (Ellen Carol Dubois and Linda Gordon 1983) whereby women must accept male dominance and then try to elevate their place within it.

Which I feel like, the way she wrote it, a lot of women might think—"oh, this isn't really a part of me, but if a man came by and cracked a whip above my head maybe I could do it" but that's like, that's not consensual. I think she just did it to try and appease him because he's mysterious and rich and so she ended up changing herself for that and that's not how it should be. (Emma)

BDSM respondents attributed Ana's lack of comfort to the lack of communication between the couple. Described by respondents as "safe, sane, consensual" it was clear that rather than engage in adult negotiation where Ana was aware of her roles and rights as a submissive, Christian practiced a devious variant of BDSM where Ana had a minimal understanding of the risks involved.

Safe, sane, consensual: "you'd never even attempt to start any kind of relationship without consent, you have to know the person consents with all activities" (Tom)

Given the extent of the activities practiced, both my interviews and observations emphasized the need for continuous and open communication described within the community as "Safe, Sane, Consensual" or RACK (Risk Aware Consensual Kink). Every person interviewed described how Safe, Sane, Consensual was essential for creating a positive environment where people could feel safe de-escalating or stopping activities quickly if they were no longer enjoying a scene. A cornerstone of this mantra, "Sane," is aimed at a partner's mental health. To be sure people are of sound mind before they get involved in a scene, many avoid alcohol and drugs that could impair judgment, especially when playing with a new partner. While consumption of mind-altering products is always a personal choice, the play parties hosted within the community I conducted my observations did not serve alcohol and many BDSM clubs noted on their websites a zero tolerance for drug use (see Figure 1).

My respondents noted that since Christian routinely offered Ana wine before engaging in sexual activity or while they discussed the contract, he violated "sane" boundaries. Veronica notes that this is a problem "if you're too drunk to consent you're too drunk to consent … it's date rapey for him to get her drunk and try to get her to agree with these things." In addition to a contract, Christian limited Ana's ability to negotiate their sexual adventures through safe words. While there was mention of a safe word in the book, James' depiction of the practice only implies a desire to stop. Framing it in this way limits the communication safe words offer, especially since many felt that Ana would not want to "stop" for fear of losing her relationship with Christian. This frames consent as "silence means yes," which is a situation inimical to BDSM culture and defies the point of safe words.

As my observations and interviews made clear, safe words aren't about "stopping": they are about checking in to see how people are enjoying the scene. Kristy, a respondent that

Figure 1. Screenhot taken from BDSM Club Website.

switches between being a dominant or a submissive depending on the relationship, describes the process "And we always check with each other … We'll be discussing something like 'you're still green on this? We're still good on this?' and I'll be like 'yeah yeah, no we're fine. We're good.'" In this way, safe words are like a spectrum, with many in the community using the colors of a traffic light: green for good/keep going, yellow for uneasiness/slow down, and red for stop. For those who I spoke with, and according to the "safe practices" seminar conducted at one of the monthly meetings I attended, getting to a point where a submissive has to say "red" should never happen because a *responsible* dominant should always check in. If a submissive says they are at yellow, a caring dominant would then slow down. In the words of one dominant, Alexandra, "I've never actually had anybody use red. That would be pretty scary if it went that far."

Constantly checking in is important, not only for the safety of the submissive but also for the dominant. For example, pro-dominant Alexandra always ties up her submissives so they can release themselves in case she might need help:

> I have double clips on everything and carabiners[10] and I never strap them to the cross or higher than they can reach. I don't have any medical conditions, but if for some reason anything should happen to me when they are laying on the table all they have to do is this (hand gesture) to unsnap it.

Moreover, safe words do not need to be vocalized. Especially when one respondent is gagged, people use sounds (like ringing a bell) or hold a ball in their hand that they drop if they need the scene to slow down or stop. In addition to individualized safety mechanisms like safe words, there are typically "dungeon monitors" at parties and clubs who monitor public play practices. As Jen and Mike recall there were a number of times they were glad there was a dungeon monitor.

> At another party where there was a rack, this guy put his bottom on the rack and the top tried to unwind him and someone came in and stopped him to let him know you have to do it slow because if you do it fast you're going to hurt him and it's good to know someone isn't going to get to crazy. (Jen)

Since "safe, sane, consensual" is such a critical element of BDSM life and given the fact that submissives are ultimately in control of dictating the kinds of sexual acts they want done to them, BDSM becomes a space where both the dominant and the submissive can consent to acts whereby they are "able to achieve equality in sexual and romantic relationships" (Fowles 2008, 119). Not only does Safe, Sane, Consensual protect the feelings of all involved; it ensures a space for "constant, enthusiastic consent" (120). None of these practices are used, or even described, in *Fifty Shades of Grey* and, in this way the narrative offers a more traditional and limiting motive of femininity and female sexual agency, emphasizing heteronormativity and positing that, as long as one person does not withdraw consent, all actions are assumed to be consensual (Angelika Tsaros 2013).

Stigma not guidance

Finally, BDSM respondents described with frustration James' connection between Christian being abused by his mother as a child and his involvement with BDSM:

> I don't feel like a majority of people in the BDSM community have a tortured past at all and I took a bit of offense that she would put that out there that that was the reason why he was into

BDSM or like anyone is like that, I mean we already have that stereotype to overcome and I feel like it's a real disservice to the community. (Zoe)

The women in the focus group echoed Zoe's sentiments—

Sarah: I hear "cured of BDSM" and to me that's the same thing as being cured of being gay.

Jane: Exactly.

Sarah: It's like No. It doesn't work like that. It's not a sickness.

So while mainstream portrayals of BDSM like *Fifty Shades* might seemingly open up the door for acceptance and understanding they do not make significant inroads because they still rely on a division of sexuality into normal/abnormal (Margot D. Weiss 2006, 119). Similar to pornographic BDSM imagery, *Fifty Shades* fails to include the essential elements of BDSM that celebrate female pleasure and empowerment and instead frame BDSM as a practice to get the dominant (often depicted as the straight male) off as quickly as possible (Riggs 2008). While *Fifty Shades* producers used the *idea* of BDSM as a marketing tool to attract women in "vanilla" relationships, they ultimately framed BDSM as a sickness, maintaining the standard that non-monogamous relationships, pornography, and sex for money are still securely contained in the "outer limits" (Barker 2013). In doing so, *Fifty Shades* entrenches the "line" between order and chaos, granting virtue to the dominant group (heterosexual couples) while "relegating vice to the underprivileged" (Rubin 1984, 14).

We see this classification of BDSM as "abnormal" in Click's (2015) findings. Fans were quick to differentiate between the "fucking" (i.e., BDSM), which they were disgusted by, and the "love-making" that they aspired to in their own relationships (Click 2015). Delineating between what types of sexual practices they would or would not "try out" with their partners was also evident in my small sample of traditional/vanilla *Fifty Shades* fans. Specifically, one respondent said that the book allowed her to open up more sexually with her husband but was clear to note that it was "not like we would try any of the bondage stuff."

However, as my data demonstrate, the "bondage stuff" is a space where women might have an opportunity to increase their own sexual agency. By providing a misguided idea of the role of the submissive and glossing over the importance of Safe, Sane, Consensual, James effectively removed the aspects of BDSM relationships that make them unique from the heteronormative standard. This is problematic because women seem to view *Fifty Shades* as an outlet for sexual frustration even though the novel maintains, rather than challenges, existing power dynamics between men and women in heterosexual relationships. The series concludes much more like a Disney movie than an exploratory manual into how BDSM can serve as a form of empowerment, ending in a fairytale depiction of Ana and Christian as married with children. Ana's love has "cured" Christian of his need for BDSM, and while they still make the occasional trip to the "red room of pain," Ana can do so while achieving traditional heterosexual respectability (Angela McRobbie 2008). Working as a form of "conservative feminism" (Dubois and Gordon 1983), *Fifty Shades* only uses BDSM as a marketing tool to legitimize and sanitize women's desire to have sex without really giving them agency to explore their sexual desires outside of the male dominated framework.

Submissive control, negotiation of boundaries, and continuous communication regarding consent all relate back to communicative acts that my BDSM respondents felt were mostly missing from most "vanilla" relationships. As they described, constantly touching base and talking about sexual desires not only opened exploration in the bedroom but also helped them resolve unrelated disagreements within their relationships. Failing to focus on

FEMINIST RECEPTION STUDIES IN A POST-AUDIENCE AGE

communication hides from public view an essential element of BDSM culture and subverts the role of the submissive from an empowered individual to the standard damsel in distress. Like its predecessor *Twilight*, the depiction of the relationship between Christian and Ana puts Ana in a position of control only if she walks away rather than opening up the possibility of finding equality through BDSM.

Given the above criticisms of the cultural phenomenon *Fifty Shades*, it seems that one of the clearest problems when it comes to navigating sexual relationships in the twenty-first century is delineating whether the person with whom you engage in sex is equally committed to the encounter. This problem can be seen across the landscape of sexuality, from exploratory vanilla "hook-ups" in college to veteran BDSM play. By centering the marginalized perspectives of BDSM participants, I have complicated the cultural heteronormative notions of sexual exploration, play, and consent put forth in *Fifty Shades*. Perhaps the need for conversations around consent is more explicit in BDSM communities specifically *because* of their marginal position; however it is clear that spaces which foster heteronormative sexual engagement (i.e., college campuses) are moving toward adopting similar policies when it comes to achieving consent.

Conclusion

Given today's sexual climate, particularly on college campuses, it is clear that women and men need help negotiating *consent* when engaging in sexual exploration. While it is unfair to assume that non-consensual acts don't occur within BDSM relationships (see Barker [2013] which discusses cases of non-consensual sex inside BDSM communities), it is clear that the framework of Safe, Sane, Consensual or RISK opens up conversations and acts as a best practices guide. Clearly some inside BDSM communities might violate trust, but unlike heteronormative sex, BDSM culture is based on the premise of open, constant, and affirmative consent. Interestingly, college campuses are starting to adopt "affirmative consent" policies as a way of combating the problem of sexual assault.[11] By adopting "affirmative consent" policies, universities outline that sexual engagement should be active, step-by-step, knowing, and voluntary.[12] However, it is unclear if those engaging in heteronormative sex know what "affirmative consent" really means or how to adopt a language of "yes means yes" during sexual encounters. While existing research indicates that *Fifty Shades* helps women navigate the hypersexualized post-feminist environment by allowing them to articulate their sexual desires (Click 2015), my research demonstrates that the narrative *does not* provide a guide for how to express sexual *limits*. While BDSM play could help fans of *Fifty Shades* learn how to constantly touch base with their partner or refrain from alcohol and drugs while playing, especially with strangers, ironically it is precisely these elements of BDSM culture that are missing from the book.

In order to make these claims, I demonstrated a need to go further with regard to what constitutes "an audience" in active audience studies. Fandom scholars like Nancy Baym (2000), Denise Bielby, C. Lee Harrington, and William Bielby (1999) and Henry Jenkins (1992) have demonstrated that audiences can interact with media objects in a myriad of ways, changing the meaning to fit their own cultural logics and even form communities around these new narratives. While this process of studying fandom is important, I argue that exclusively studying "fans" with regard to audience analysis can be limiting. The concept of "convergence culture" (Henry Jenkins 2006) can empower fragmented audiences to collaborate on new narratives, but existing studies fail to consider how some audiences might not be afforded the same opportunities to participate. *Fifty Shades* is a perfect example. In an era when production and consumption are increasingly intertwined (George Ritzer and Nathan Jurgenson 2010), the clear separation between the creator and subject of *Fifty Shades* is archaically static. Even though *Fifty Shades* is a product of "convergence culture,"[13] the BDSM audience was not "integrated" in the creation of the product, despite the ease with which James could have connected with the community using Reddit's BDSM subreddit page, Wikipedia, alt.com, or reading prominent BDSM blogs. While *Fifty Shades* might have empowered *Twilight* fans (James in particular), my findings demonstrate that a lack of BDSM representation further stigmatizes BDSM culture as "non-normative." Forging new inquires into what constitutes an audience and how audiences are increasingly integrated (or not) allows researchers to incorporate a sociological perspective that aims to understand how media forms represent and misrepresent particular groups. Future research on "integrated audiences" provides a space where scholars can investigate how media intersects with *community* representation, influencing group identity, and, at times, transforming it.[14]

By utilizing my concept of an "integrated audience," we can also expand on how existing research on *Fifty Shades* fails to examine the *implications* of hiding from the public important aspects of BDSM culture and the implications of maintaining that separation. What I argue is that James' lack of interaction and engagement with existing BDSM communities ultimately provides a disservice for women seeking a resource for the confusing sexual environment they are currently living in. By opening up for discussion the implications of failing to integrate the BDSM community into the creation of *Fifty Shades,* this paper demonstrates how the mainstream depiction of BDSM falls dramatically short of BDSM lived experiences. Failure to understand a woman's power in a sexual relationship, failure to communicate sexual desires while not under the influence of drugs and alcohol, and failure to obtain clear consent are all missing from this wildly fantastical depiction of BDSM life. Not only does James' depiction of BDSM as a mental disease work as a disservice to the BDSM community, her novel also fails to educate "vanilla" readers on the most important aspect of BDSM culture—affirmative consent. Future research could investigate these connections, paying particular attention to the elements of BDSM outlined in this paper and how failure to discuss sexual desires both before and during sex might be linked to the prevalent problem of sexual assault on college campuses.

Notes

1. Merchandise includes a vibrator, handcuffs, a blindfold, a cock-ring and the aforementioned Ben Wa Balls. Available at: http://www.babeland.com/bondage-fifty-shades-of-grey/l/34 (last accessed June 6, 2016).
2. Many have made the connection online describing it as "50 Shades of Abuse"—here are links to a few of these articles available online, although this is not an exhaustive list: <http://everydayfeminism.com/2015/03/50-shades-of-abuse-10-signs-of-unhealthy-relationships-a-la-christian-grey/>, <http://www.huffingtonpost.com/elisabeth-corey/50-shades-of-abuse_b_6735520.html>, <https://www.washingtonpost.com/posteverything/wp/2015/02/13/there-is-a-line-between-dominance-and-abuse-and-fifty-shades-of-grey-is-blurring-it/>, <https://twitter.com/50shadesabuse?ref_src=twsrc%5Egoogle%7Ctwcamp%5Eserp%7Ctwgr%5Eauthor>.
3. Feminist scholarship on female audience is not exclusive to romance novels. In addition to those mentioned above studies on feminized media texts have looked at women's magazines, soap operas, and chick-lit.

4. These focus groups were conducted with Andrea Press as part of a larger study on twenty-first century feminism. The women ranged from late twenties to early thirties and approximately 60 percent of them were married with all of them identifying as heterosexual. Based on their affiliation with a prominent women's group, it was clear that they were all affluent.

5. While Radway does not specifically state that the readers of "Smithton" are heterosexual, they are all women who are married women who work primarily as housewives. In Click's most recent study on *Fifty Shades* readers, 92 percent of those she interviewed identified as heterosexual.

6. This paper is not meant to only address the problems of non-consensual sex within hook-up culture on college campuses. Even though college women "are at greater risk for rape and other forms of sexual assault than women in the general population or in a comparable age group" (Bonnie Fisher, Francis Cullen, and Michael Turner 2000), it is clear that women who have graduated (or never been) to college are also navigating the question of consent when hooking-up with new partners. For more details regarding the results of the survey visit <https://www.aau.edu/Climate-Survey.aspx?id=16525>.

7. Most communities have membership fees. In addition, toys, conferences, and hosting play parties are all expensive. While people I spoke with ranged in terms of income, I would argue that those hovering around the poverty line would have a difficult time affording the costs associated with BDSM play. One of my respondents, Jon, echoed this sentiment, noting that many people like him "who make a modest income aren't very active because they can't afford it."

8. To protect the confidentiality of those who participated in this study all names have been changed and specific geographic locations are not used.

9. Limited knowledge regarding safe practices was also reported by Consumer Safety Reports which found that trips to the emergency room involving sex toys doubled following the release of *Fifty Shades* (2012–2013)—83 percent of which required the removal of foreign bodies.

10. Carabiners are widely used in rope-intensive activities such as climbing, arboriculture, caving, sailing, hot air ballooning, rope rescue, construction, industrial rope work, window cleaning, whitewater rescue, and acrobatics. They are predominantly made from both steel and aluminum. Those used in sports tend to be of a lighter weight than those used in commercial applications and rope rescue.

11. As of 2014, over eight hundred schools had adopted "affirmative consent" policies. See this website for full listing and more information: <https://www.insidehighered.com/news/2014/10/17/colleges-across-country-adopting-affirmative-consent-sexual-assault-policies>.

12. Take, for example, the affirmative consent policy put in place at the University of Virginia in 2015: <http://www.virginia.edu/sexualviolence/sexualassault/consent.html>.

13. EL James original book was titled "Master of the Universe" and was initially published on FanFiction.net. This book was inspired by Stephanie Meyer's *Twilight* series.

14. In addition to my work within the BDSM community, I am currently working on another article studying "integrated audiences" in a rural Louisiana town. This community is the focus of the Reality Television series *Swamp People* and I find that because community members interact with the depiction of the reality series more frequently than those in their community who hunt alligator it is framing the profession as distinctly masculine, even though women are actively involved in the business. The concept of "integrated audiences" is also the focus of my dissertation where I examine two other cases: Yik Yak and Wikipedia.

Disclosure statement

No potential conflict of interest was reported by the author.

References

Abrams, Rachel. 2015. "Sex Toy Shops Prepare for Tie-Ins to 'Fifty Shades of Grey.'" *The New York Times*. Accessed June 30, 2016. http://www.nytimes.com/2015/02/02/business/media/50-shades-of-green-shops-prepare-for-tie-ins-to-fifty-shades-of-grey-film.html?_r=2

Ang, Ien. 1991. *Desperately Seeking the Audience*. New York, NY: Routledge.

Armstrong, Elizabeth, Laura Hamilton, and Brian Sweeney. 2006. "Sexual Assault on Campus: A Multilevel, Integrative Approach to Party Rape." *Social Problems*. 53 (1): 483–499.

Barker, Meg. 2013. "Consent is a grey area? A Comparison of Understandings of Consent in *Fifty Shades of Grey* and on the BDSM Blogosphere." *Sexualities*. 16 (8): 896–914.

Baym, Nancy. 2000. *Tune In, Log On: Soaps, Fandom, and Online Community*. London: Sage Publications Inc.

Bielby, Denise, C. Lee Harrington, and William Bielby. 1999. "Whose Stories are They? Fans' Engagement with Soap Opera Narratives in Three Sites of Fan Activity." *Journal of Broadcasting and Electronic Media* 43 (1): 35–51.

Bosman, Julie. 2014. "For 'Fifty Shades of Grey,' More than 100 Million Sold." *The New York Times*. Accessed May 25, 2016. http://www.nytimes.com/2014/02/27/business/media/for-fifty-shades-of-grey-more-than-100-million-sold.html?_r=0

Charmaz, Kathy. 2006. *Constructing Grounded Theory : A Practical Guide through Qualitative Analysis*. Thousand Oaks, CA: Sage Publications.

Click, Melissa. 2015. "*Fifty Shades* of Postfeminism: Contextualizing Readers' Reflection on the Erotic Romance Series." In *Cupcakes, Pinterest, and Ladyporn. Feminized Popular Culture in the Early Twenty-First Centry*, edited by Elana Levine, 15–31. Illinois: University of Illinois Press.

Douglas, Susan. 2010. *The Rise of Enlightened Sexism*. New York, NY: St. Martin's Press.

Dubois, Ellen Carol, and Linda Gordon. 1983. "Seeking Ecstasy on the Battlefield: Danger and Pleasure in Nineteenth-Century Feminist Sexual Thought." *Feminist Studies*. 9 (1): 7–25.

Fisher, Bonnie, Francis Cullen, and Michael Turner. 2000. *The Sexual Victimization of College Women*. Washington, DC: National Institute of Justice and the Bureau of Justice Statistics. https://www.ncjrs.gov/pdffiles1/nij/182369.pdf

Fowles, Stacy May. 2008. "The Fantasy of Acceptable 'Non-Consent': Why the Female Sexual Submissive Scares us (and why she Shouldn't)." In *Yes Means Yes: Visions of Female Sexual Power and a World Without Rape*, edited by Jessica Valenti and Jaclyn Friedman, 117–125. Berkeley, CA: Seal Press.

Gill, Rosalind. 2007. "Postfeminist Media Culture: Elements of a Sensibility." *European Journal of Cultural Studies*. 10 (2): 147–166.

Illouz, Eva. 2014. *Hard-Core Romance: "Fifty Shades of Grey", Best-Sellers, and Society*. Chicago, IL: University of Chicago Press.

James, E. L. 2011. *Fifty Shades of Grey*. New York: Vintage Books – Random House.

Jenkins, Henry. 1992. *Textual Poachers: television fans and participatory culture*. New York, NY: Routledge.

Jenkins, Henry. 2006. *Convergence culture: where old and new media collide*. New York, NY: NYU Press.

Lang, Brent. 2015. "Box Office: 'Fifty Shades of Grey' Explodes with Record-Breaking $81.7 Million." *Variety*. Accessed June 06, 2016. http://variety.com/2015/film/news/box-office-fifty-shades-of-grey-explodes-with-record-breaking-81-7-million-1201434486

Liebes, Tamar, and Elihu Katz. 1990. *The Export of Meaning: Cross-Cultural Readings of Dallas*. New York, NY: Oxford University Press.

McRobbie, Angela. 2008. *The Aftermath of Feminism: Gender*. Culture and Social Change: Sage Publications.

Press, Andrea. 1991. *Women watching television: gender, class, and generation in the American television experience*. Pennsylvania: University of Pennsylvania Press.

Radway, Janice. 1984. *Reading The Romance: Women, Patriarch, and Popular Literature*. Chapel Hill: University of NC Press.

Riggs, Lee Jacobs. 2008. "A Love Letter from an Anti-Rape Activist to Her Feminist Sex-Toy Store." In *Yes Means Yes: Visions of Female Sexual Power and a World Without Rape*, edited by Jessica Valenti and Jaclyn Friedman Berkeley, 107–117. CA: Seal Press.

Ritzer, George, and Nathan Jurgenson. 2010. "Production, Consumption, Prosumption. The nature of capitalism in the age of the digital 'prosumer.'" *Journal of Consumer Culture* 10 (1): 13–36.

Rubin, Gayle. 1984. "Thinking Sex: Notes for a Radical Theory of the Politics of Sexuality." In *From Gender to Sexuality*, 143–178. http://sites.middlebury.edu/sexandsociety/files/2015/01/Rubin-Thinking-Sex.pdf

Thurston, Carol. 1987. *The Romance Revolution: Erotic Novels and the Quest for a New Sexual Identity*. Chicago, IL: University of Illinois Press.

Tsaros, Angelika. 2013. "Consensual non-consent: Comparing EL James's *Fifty Shades of Grey* and Pauline Reage's *Story of O.*" *Sexualities*. 16 (8): 864–879.

Weiss, Margot D. 2006. "Mainstreaming kink: The politics of BDSM representation in US popular media." In *Sadomasochism: Powerful Pleasures*, edited by Peggy Kleinplatz and Charles Moser, 103–132. Binghampton, NY: Harrington Press.

Wilkinson, Eleanor. 2009. "Perverting visual pleasure: Representing sadomasochism." *Sexualities*. 12 (2): 181–198.

van Zoonen, Liesbet. 1994. *Feminist Media Studies*. London: Sage Publications.

Index

Note: Italic page numbers refer to figures, pagenumbers followed by "n" denote endnotes.

ACB *see* Anonymous Confession Board
AcidJazz, Banty 66, 67
affective authenticity 85
affirmative consent policy 103, 105n11
Ally McBeal 16
Anderson, Karrin Vasby 17
Anonymous Confession Board (ACB) 10
anti-feminism 16
anti-fluoridation activism 67
anti-vaxers 66–9 *see also* pro-vaxers
a priori delineations 80
Armstrong, Elizabeth 99
Association of American Universities 96
asymmetrical gender system 46
authenticity 89; affective 85; gender and 86; online self-presentation and 85

Barad, Karen 80, 85
Bauwel, Sofie Van 3
Baym, Nancy 103
BDSM *see* bondage, discipline, and sadomasochism
Belkin, Lisa 62
Bielby, Denise 103
Bielby, William 103
Biltereyst, Daniel 3
blogs, mothers and 61–3
bondage, discipline, and sadomasochism (BDSM) 10; classification of 102; Club Website *100*; community 96, 97, 104, 105n7, 105n14; culture 104; *Fifty Shades'* portrayal of 94, 101–3; relationships 94, 102; respondents 97–100; "safe, sane, consensual" 94, 100–1
Bore, Inger-Lise Kalviknes 21
Bronstein, Carolyn 9
Brown, Mary Ellen 94
Butler, Judith 78
Byerly, Carolyn M. 1

camera glitches 83–6
Cavalcante, Andre 4, 9
cellphone 79, 88; camera glitches 83–6; invariants 79; as mirror 82–3; multi-stabilities of 82
Chappelle, Dave 17; *see also* selfies
childhood vaccination 61
China: asymmetrical gender system 46; female homoeroticism 49; hetero-patriarchal expectations 50; homonormative culture 46; homosexual-friendly 45; homosexuality in universities 46; lesbian culture 45–6; non-heterosexuality 46; shock therapy 46
Chinese cyberspace 43
Chinese fans' queer gossip 42–3; GE gossip 43–4; queer normalization 45–7
Click, Melissa 95, 105n5
Cole, Elizabeth R. 3
Comedy Central 17
conservative feminism 99
convergence culture 6, 103–4
cultural valorization, of Denmark 49

Das, Ranjana 77
de Beauvoir, Simone 4
De Lauretis, Teresa 35, 36
Dell'Antonia, KJ 62, 64–7, 69–71
Deuze, Mark 77
Dhaenens, Frederik 3
digital dualism 80, 89
digital technologies 79
"disidentification" idea 4
Doty, Alexander 3
Douai, Aziz 7
drug trafficking 29, 33
Dunham, Lena 15, 16

Ellis, John 7
Erichsen, Freja Beha 43; "god-like nation" 49; homoerotic pictures 47; homosocial/homoerotic relationships 43; intimate pictures of 49; lasting tomboyism 51; lesbian identity 47, 48; lesbianism 44, 51, 54;

INDEX

lesbian romance 51; "little prince" 49; media celebration and commercialization 43; "prince from a fairytale kingdom" 48–9; romantic and sexual relationships 49; SMILE-VIVI 50, 51; *Tale of a Fairy, The* 47, *47*

"everyday world as problematic" (Smith) 4

Facebook™ 78, 86
female homoeroticism 49
female romance readers 2
"feminist agenda" 22
feminist audience study 1; contemporary media environment 4–6; genres 3; interrogation of everyday life 1–4; qualitative methods in 6–10; queer audience research 3; tradition of 2–3
feminist humor 17–18
feminist media studies 1, 2, 42
"feminist methodology" 3
feminist new materialism 80–1
feminist scholarship 94, 104n3
Fey, Tina 14, 15
Fifty Shades 93–4; active audience research 95–7, 103; affirmative consent policies 103, 105n11; Click's findings 95, 105n5; conservative feminism 99; convergence culture 103–4; criticisms of 94; cultural prominence 94; feminist scholarship 94, 104n3; and film adaptation 97; Illouz's theory 95; "integrated audiences" 104, 105n14; interest and identity 97–8; merchandise 97, 104n1; popularity of 97; "safe practices" scenario 97; "self help" book 94–6; sexual autonomy 95–6; submissive power 98–100; *see also* bondage, discipline, and sadomasochism
"50 Shades of Abuse" 104n2
Fifty Shades of Grey 5–6, 10, 93–4
Flores, Blanca 32
foreplay 80, 82, 83
Fowles, Stacy May 98
freedom, moral status of 68
free-range parenting 61; vaccination and 60, 65, 68
Friedan, Betty 4

Gajjala, Radhike 9
Garden of Eden Communication Site for Foreign Series (GE) 42, 43; Erichsen, Freja Beha 43, *44*; lesbian family 51–4; online surveys 43; tomboyism 48–51; Western lesbian imaginary 47–8
gender, feminism and comedy 20–3
gender identities 32
Gestalt shift 79
Gill, Rosalind 17
Girls 15, 16, 19, 20, 22, 25
glitches 78; camera 83–6; mirror 82–3

glitch feminism 78–9, 85, 89; camera glitches 83–6; feminist new materialism and 80–1; mirror glitches 82–3; post-phenomenology and 79; social media glitches 86–7; *see also* selfies
"global gay" theory 43
Google™ chat 9, 82
Grace, Daniel 8, 10
Gray, Frances 17
Gray, Mary L. 8–9

Hamilton, Laura 99
Hankivsky, Olena 8, 10
Harper, Douglas 81
Harrington, C. Lee 103
"helicopter" parenting 61, 69
Hermes, Joke O. K. E. 1
Herzog, Herta 1–2; everyday life 2–3; radio soap operas 2
hetero-marital harmony 49
heteronormative social environment 50
heterosexual identity 34, 36
heterosexuality 4, 32, 38, 50
heterosexual original 50
heterosexual proxy, Piper Chapman as 31–7
Hobson, Dorothy 4, 94
homosexuality 45, 46
Huffington Post, The 61

Illouz's theory 95
imagined audience 78, 86, 87
individual freedom 68
Instagram™ 86, 87
"integrated audiences" 104, 105n14
intensive mothering 60, 63
intensive parenting 60, 64, 65, 69, 72
inter-action 80
Internet: field research methods 64; on-demand streaming service 30, 39n2; theorists of 77
intra-action 80
investment parenting 63
IPhone4™ 83

James, E. L. 93, 105n13
Jenkins, Henry 10, 103
Jing Jamie Zhao 9
Jurgensen, Nathan 80

Kaling, Mindy 15–16
Kodak Brownie™ 83
Kohan, Jenji 30, 31

Lagerfeld, Karl 48; *Remember Now* 47; Spring 2011 Chanel campaign 48
Lancet, The 61
language 45, 98; style and 66–8
Lefebvre, Henri 4
Lemish, Dafna 17

INDEX

lesbian culture: in China 45–6; public visibility and awareness 46
lesbianism 49–51
lesbian marriage 52
lesbian sexual expression 32
lesbian sexuality 31, 33, 34, 36–8
Lindlof, Thomas R. 7
Livingstone, Sonia 7, 9, 77
Lorde, Audre 4

Markham, Annette N. 7, 9
mass archiving 7
McNeil, Catherine 51, 52
McRobbie, Angela 16, 94
measles–mumps–rubella (MMR) 61, 64, 66–7, 69
media environment, challenge of 4–6; ethnographic methods 9; multi-sitedness of 5
media life: boundaries for 8; demotic turn in 5; people's engagement with 7; research 6; technological character of 5
Mellencamp, Patricia 25
Mindy Project, The 15–16, 19, 25
mirror glitches 82–3
Mizejewski, Linda 17
MMR see measles–mumps–rubella
Modleski, Tania 1, 4
mommyblogs 62; method 64–5; parenting 62
"mommy wars" 63
Morello, Lorna 32
Moroccan news media audiences 7
mothering 59, 60; standards of 61
Motherlode 60–2, 65; Belkin, Lisa 62; community's sense 68; free-range parenting 69–72; as political space 72; style and language 66–8
mothers, roles of blogs 61–3
multi-sited media environments 7
multi-staged project 10
Muñoz, José Esteban 4
Muse, Arizona 51, 52
MySpace 84

Navar-Gill, Annemarie 7
Negra, Diane 16
neoliberal individualism 68
neoliberalism 59, 60; investment parenting 63; risk managment 63–4
neoliberal mothering 65
neoliberal parenting 9, 66; and risk management 63–4
news cycle sensationalism 72
news media, parents' critique of 72–3
New York Sun 61
New York Times 60, 62, 72
Nichols, Nicky 32; sexual liaisons 36; sexual relationship 34, 36
normative heterosexuality 38, 49–50

offline lesbian social gatherings 45
"On Borrowed Experience: An Analysis of Listening to Daytime Sketches" (Herzog) 1–2
online lesbian communicative spaces 45
online self-presentation, authenticity and 85
online spaces 8
Orange Is the New Black (OITNB) 9, 29; commercial viability 31; Flores, Blanca 32; invitational structure 31; Kohan, Jenji 30, 31; lesbian characters 30; Morello, Lorna 32; Nichols, Nicky 32; Piper Chapman 29; queer sexuality in 36; same-sex encounters 34; sexual/identity tourism 31, 34; straight-identified audiences 35; straight-identified women 30–5, 38; Vause, Alex 29; voyeurism 31, 33–8

Parameswaran, Radhika 7, 8
parenting: blogs 61, 62, 64; "helicopter" 61, 69; intensive 60, 64, 65, 69, 72; investment 63; neoliberal 9, 63–4, 66; see also free-range parenting
Parks and Recreation 14–15, 18, 19, 21, 25
personal freedom 68
photo elicitation: with post-phenomenological analysis 81–2; variation of 81
Piper Chapman 9, 29; Chickening, The 33; drug trafficking conviction 29; enculturation 35; eye-line 32–4; heterosexual proxy 31–5, 37–8; lesbian sexuality 33; "not still a lesbian" 32; prison life 32; queer sexuality 31; same-sex encounters 33; sexual ambiguity 37; sexual/identity tourism 31, 34; sexual orientation 34; straight-identified women differently 30–5, 38; voyeuristic position 37
Poehler, Amy 14, 15
popularization of queer content 29, 31
post-feminism, comedy and media 16–17
post-feminist humor 17–18
"postfeminist sensibility" 95
post-phenomenology 90n1; authenticity 85; glitch feminism and 79; multi-stable technology 78; photo elicitation with 81–2
post-representational approach 80
Press, Andrea L. 3, 7, 10
"problem that has no name" (Friedan) 4
pro-vaxers 67–9

qualitative audience studies 1
queer audiences 3–4
queer normalization 45–7
queer sensibility, acquisition of 3, 36–8
queer sexuality 30–1, 35, 36, 38
queer theory 3
queer women: gender and sexuality 48; self-conflicting aspirations 46; self-expression 46; social roles of 45; socio-cultural situations 45; survival and expression 42; tactical negotiations 46

INDEX

RACK *see* Risk Aware Consensual Kink
radio soap operas 2
Radway, Janice 2–3, 94, 105n5
Remember Now 47
representationalism 80
Riggs, Lee Jacobs 98
Risk Aware Consensual Kink (RACK) 100
romance novels: housewives 95; Radway's
    research on 94; sexual agency 94
Rose, Gillian 9
Rose, Ruby 52
Russell, Jan Jarboe 63
Russell, Legacy 80

Salamon, Gayle 86, 89
same-sex couplings 34
same-sex desire: experience of 35–7; feelings of
    33, 34; Piper's queering 33; straight-identified
    women's experience 33, 34
Scannell, Paddy 4
science, status of 68–9
"second sex" (de Beauvoir) 4
selfies 9, 77–8; glitch feminism; cellphone as
    camera 83; as embodiment 78; good 88;
    limitations 88; post-phenomenological
    phenomenon 78–9; as presentation 78;
    as representation 78, 84, 85; specificity of
    audience 87; taking process 82; *see also*
    cellphone
Sender, Katherine 10
Sex and the City 16
sexual assault 96; on college campuses 99, 105n6
sexual identity 29, 32–3
sexual/identity tourism 31, 34
sexual orientation 33
sexual permissiveness 49
Shaw, Adrienne 9
Sheeler, Kristina Horn 17
Shifman, Limor 17
shock therapy 46
Silverstone, Roger 4
"sister outsider" (Lorde) 4
Skeggs, Beverley 10
Smith, Dorothy 4
Snapchat™ 86, 87
social identity 34, 35
social media glitches 86–7
Sony Erikson z1010™ 82
space–time–matterings 85
spectatorial positioning, specificity of
    35–6, 39n8

Spigel, Lynn 4–5
Steiner, Linda 9
straight-identified women 30–5, 38
Sundén, Jenny 80, 89
Sweeney, Brian 99
Swink, Robyn 9
Symes, Katarina 9

Tale of a Fairy, The 47, *47*
Taylor, Bryan C. 7
television 4; availability, radical transformation
    in 7; post-war domestic life and 5; soap
    operas 3, 4
television comedies and feminism 14–15;
    Ally McBeal 16; ambivalent enjoyment
    19–20; *Comedy Central* 17; Dunham, Lena
    15, 16; "feminist agenda" 22; feminist *vs.*
    post-feminist humor 17–18; Fey, Tina
    14, 15; gender, feminism, and comedy
    20–3; *Girls* 15, 16, 19, 20, 22, 25; Kaling,
    Mindy 15–16; *Mindy Project, The* 15–16,
    19; *Parks and Recreation* 14–15, 18, 19, 21,
    25; participants' perceptions of 18–19, 23;
    Poehler, Amy 14, 15; politics, feelings, and
    post-feminist representations 23–5;
    post-feminism 16–17; research questions
    15; *Sex and the City* 16; *30 Rock* 14, 15,
    18–21, 24, 25
Texas Monthly 63
30 Rock 14, 15, 18–21, 24, 25
Thurston, Carol 94
tomboyism 48, 50, 51
Tripodi, Francesca 10
Tumblr™ 78
Turner, Graeme 5
Twilight 93, 103

vaccination 65–6, 73n6; childhood 61; criticisms
    of 61; forced 68; and "free-range" parenting
    60, 65, 68; measles 61
Vause, Alex 29
voyeurism 31, 33–8

Warfield, Katie 9
Washington Post 63, 69
Wellner, Galit P. 79, 83, 88
Western lesbian imaginary 47–8
women's humor 17 *see also* television comedies
    and feminism
"women's time" 1
Wood, Helen 10